LIVING

AS AN

OVERCOMER

TONY EVANS

HARVEST HOUSE PUBLISHERS
EUGENE. OREGON

Unless otherwise indicated, all Scripture verses are taken from the (NASB®) New American Standard Bible®, Copyright © 1960, 1971, 1977, 1995 by The Lockman Foundation. Used by permission. All rights reserved. www.lockman.org.

Verses marked NKJV are taken the New King James Version®. Copyright © 1982 by Thomas Nelson. Used by permission. All rights reserved.

Cover design by Studio Gearbox

Cover images © White_Engine, FMStox / Shutterstock

Interior design by KUHN Design Group

Some content in chapter 1, "The Key to Overcoming," is adapted from Tony Evans, *The Kingdom Agenda* (Chicago, IL: Moody Publishers, 2013). Used with permission.

Some content in chapter 9, "Obtaining Power for Spiritual Battle," is adapted from Tony Evans, *Kingdom Citizen* (Carol Stream, IL: Tyndale House Publishers, 2018). Used with permission.

Some content in chapter 10, "Living as a Conqueror in All Things," is adapted from Tony Evans, *The Power of the Cross* (Chicago, IL: Moody Publishers, 2016). Used with permission.

For bulk, special sales, or ministry purchases, please call 1-800-547-8979.
Email: Customerservice@hhpbooks.com

This logo is a federally registered trademark of the Hawkins Children's LLC. Harvest House Publishers, Inc., is the exclusive licensee of this trademark.

Living as an Overcomer
Copyright © 2023 by Tony Evans
Published by Harvest House Publishers
Eugene, Oregon 97408
www.harvesthousepublishers.com

ISBN 978-0-7369-7528-5 (pbk)
ISBN 978-0-7369-7529-2 (eBook)

Library of Congress Control Number: 2021937788

Printed in the United States of America

23 24 25 26 27 28 29 30 31 / BP / 10 9 8 7 6 5 4 3 2 1

ACKNOWLEDGMENTS

I want to thank my friends at Harvest House Publishers for their long-standing partnership in bringing my thoughts, study, and words to print. I particularly want to thank Bob Hawkins for his friendship over the years, as well as his pursuit of excellence in leading his company. I also want to publicly thank Kim Moore and Jean Bloom for their help in the editorial process. In addition, my appreciation goes out to Heather Hair for her skills and insights in collaboration on this manuscript.

CONTENTS

Introduction: A Call to Overcome 7

PART ONE: WHERE TO BEGIN

1. The Key to Overcoming 11

PART TWO: JESUS' MESSAGES
TO THE SEVEN CHURCHES

2. Putting God in First Place 29

3. Exhibiting Steady Faithfulness 45

4. Embracing Uncompromising Commitment 57

5. Viewing Sin God's Way 71

6. Walking in the Spirit's Power 85

7. Accessing Spiritual Authority 103

8. Reflecting Authentic Christianity 117

PART THREE: CHOICES TO MAKE

9. Obtaining Power for Spiritual Battle 135

10. Living as a Conqueror in All Things 151

11. Pursuing a Godly Life 165

12. Rejoicing in Growth and Abundance 179

Conclusion: From Victim to Victor 191

Appendix A: Scriptures for Encouragement to Overcome . . . 195

Appendix B: The Urban Alternative 205

A CALL TO OVERCOME

Two of the premiere events in track and field are the high jump and pole vault, and both present the same challenge for the athletes: They're trying to hurl themselves over an elevated bar without knocking it down. A good male high jumper can propel himself over eight feet. A good male pole vaulter, on the other hand, can propel himself over 18 feet. The difference between the two is what they have to work with. The high jumper is totally dependent on his own leg strength, skill, stamina, and training to overcome the height of the bar. The pole vaulter, however, also uses a flexible pole to help hurl himself over the even greater height before him.

Our lives are full of all types of challenges seeking to defeat us—difficulties, problems, sin, circumstances, trials—and many Christians find themselves unable to deal with them. They come up short, knocking down the "bar" in front of them because their human effort, abilities, and strength are insufficient to transcend their trouble. They can't soar high enough on their own. So instead of enjoying the thrill of victory, they're constantly enduring the agony of defeat. They haven't done what's necessary to overcome.

The good news is that God, through the person and work of His Son, Jesus Christ, has given every believer the tools necessary to be an overcomer. He has provided the position, power, and protocol we need to be victorious so we don't have to live perpetually defeated. Rather, victory is within our reach as we latch on to the One who has already overcome all on behalf of the world and each of us.

Sometimes we don't recognize God's provision, though. Or we get so caught up in our problems that we miss noticing His sovereign hand. That's why it's important to regularly study the Scriptures and learn from those who have gone before us. The Bible isn't just a collection of stories designed to make us feel good. Rather, it's the voice of God in print, and He uses the stories and principles in His Word for our benefit today. When we set out to study Scripture, there's always an application that relates to us both collectively and individually—as long as we ask God to reveal it.

Studying the seven churches Jesus addressed in the book of Revelation—located in the ancient cities of Ephesus, Smyrna, Pergamum, Thyatira, Sardis, Philadelphia, and Laodicea—is no different. That's why I've produced this book and an accompanying small-group video series based on sermons I preached at the church where I pastor. I want you to get to know each church individually and then allow the truths revealed concerning their members to help you live as an overcomer in your own church and in the world around you. In addition, I want you to understand how you will be rewarded in eternity as an overcomer.

All that is what *Living as an Overcomer* is about.

PART ONE

WHERE TO BEGIN

Before we dive into the messages Jesus sent to the seven churches in Revelation 2 and 3, we need to understand some foundational concepts and answer some relevant questions. What is the key to becoming an overcomer? What is spiritual independence, and why is it so detrimental for us? What's special about the number seven we see over and over in Revelation? What does it mean to hear? Have we already overcome, or do we still need to overcome? There's more, but let's get started.

THE KEY TO OVERCOMING

We all have challenges to overcome—difficult circumstances, disturbing emotions, detrimental habits, or hard situations that hold us back. But to live as an overcomer is more about how to face these adversities than about avoiding them. Overcoming is not a blueprint to a daily utopia. Rather, it's a map for how to rise above the challenges thrown at us. Overcoming is not an event; it's a lifestyle. We live as an overcomer when the principles we examine in this book regularly operate in our heart and life. And when we live according to these principles, we're already victors by the power of Christ's kingdom authority.

But if that's true, why on earth do we seem to still be in a battle? And what keeps us from adopting the lifestyle of an overcomer?

SPIRITUAL INDEPENDENCE

The annual Independence Day celebration in our nation ushers in a time of rest, enjoyment, great food, and even greater displays of fireworks. But let's focus on another type of independence—what I call spiritual independence. If you have named Christ as your one and only God and Savior, you have declared independence from the rule of sin and Satan over your life. You've been set free. As Colossians 1:13 tells us, "[God] rescued us from the domain of darkness, and transferred us to the kingdom of His beloved Son."

Having gained spiritual independence from the rule of Satan, you may be wondering why, then, it often feels like you're still in a battle. Just like the British didn't allow its American colonies to secure their freedom simply by asking for it or letting them just declare it, Satan is not about to let you go without putting up his opposition. He knows that if he lets you out from under his influence, you become dangerous to his agenda. Instead of his telling you what to do, you'll be telling him what you're going to do.

That doesn't sit well with Satan at all. Even though Jesus has legally, under His law, set you free from the reign of sin in your life, the devil doesn't want you to be experientially set free. It's one thing to have the status of freedom; it's another thing entirely to experience it. But the truth in God's Word can help you walk into the full realization and experience of spiritual freedom.

In the book of Revelation, the apostle John tells us how Jesus sent a message to each of the seven churches of Asia Minor, addressing this concept of complete spiritual freedom in multiple ways. And the number seven comes into play over and over again.

WHAT'S IN A NUMBER?

In the Bible, the number seven represents completeness and fullness as well as to signify perfection, and it comes up regularly throughout the book of Revelation:

- seven churches (1:4, 11, 20)
- seven golden lampstands (1:12-13, 20; 2:1)
- seven stars (1:16, 20; 2:1; 3:1)
- seven spirits (1:4; 3:1; 4:5; 5:6)

- seven lamps (4:5)
- seven seals (5:1, 5)
- seven horns (5:6)

These are just a few of the many mentions of seven in Revelation. And sometimes when that number is used in Scripture, it means something *hasn't* reached its full expression. So from these passages with messages to the seven churches, we can infer that Jesus wants them all to be complete, fulfilled, and not lacking. He gives each of them a unique message, yes, but also as though He's saying to them as a group, "If you overcome in these seven areas, you will have overcome completely and perfectly. You will be living out the complete and abundant life I came to supply rather than the life of defeat Satan offers" (see John 10:9-10).

Even though each of these churches had its own uniqueness, problems, pressures, and burdens, Jesus' messages to them were actually very much the same. And this is why even though each of you will approach this topic of overcoming with different needs and issues—emotional, physical, circumstantial, relational, financial, career-based, or anything else—the solution rests in the same concept.

And while the specificity of everyone's situation will need to be addressed differently, the overarching solution lies in this one approach for us all: "He who has an ear, let him hear what the Spirit says to the churches" (Revelation 2:7, 11, 17, 29; 3:6, 13, 22). There again, Jesus speaks to the "churches" as a whole.

WHAT IT MEANS TO HEAR

Seven times Christ says the same exact thing to these churches: "He who has an ear, let him hear what the Spirit says." Every one of His messages—although each is addressed to a different group with a different set of problems—boils down to this same solution. Jesus suggests that it's possible to have an ear and not hear. It's possible to read and study the Word and still not receive and understand the truth. He's saying that whoever has the capacity to receive the data ought to heed and apply it rather than just acknowledge it. Because hearing with the ear has as its goal the heeding and application of the truth.

We've all talked to people who hear our words yet don't hear our message. Jesus is saying to the person who has an external ear, "Hear the internal message of what the Spirit of God is saying." The church is made up of individual people, and so although Jesus has one message for the whole congregation, it's also for each person who has an ear. In other words, each individual must decide whether they'll personally pay attention to the message—really hear it—allowing the Holy Spirit to speak to them directly.

Attending church services or even a small group won't get the truth of God deep within your spirit. Only when you choose to really hear and apply His truth will the fruit of it—the ability to overcome—be made manifest in your life. It's this ability that moves you from "We *shall* overcome," the statement often heard during the height of the civil rights movement, to "We *have* overcome," the truth of God's Word for believers.

OVERCOMING—THE HAVE AND THE WILL

First John 5 emphasizes that we *have* overcome: "Whatever is born of God overcomes the world; and this is the victory that has overcome the world—our faith. Who is the one who overcomes the world, but he who believes that Jesus is the Son of God?" (verses 4-5). So John is saying that we, victors in Christ because of our faith in Him, have already overcome. But the interesting thing is that more than once in the book of Revelation, he indicates that we *shall* overcome, using the word *will* (see 2:7, 11, 17, 26; 3:5, 12). Not *have. Will.* In other words, we still *need* to overcome.

So on one hand, then, you *have* overcome, yet on the other hand, you still *need* to overcome. We all do. Even though victory in Christ is already secured for us, in this life there will still be temptations and trials to overcome. Jesus Himself acknowledged this (John 16:33).

The Greek word used for "overcome" in this passage is *nikeo*. It means "to prevail" or "to win one's cause." It has to do with being victorious in the midst of and even through whatever difficult circumstances you're facing. It assumes some challenge or adversity is seeking to defeat you. Thus, if you have something illegitimately holding you hostage—emotional, circumstantial, relational, spiritual, or physical—you can overcome it. That is, to prevail and come out as a victor in your life. To access the power available to you.

Life is a participatory experience, though, so we get to choose what power we tap into and what we overcome. God has made the *nikeo* available to us, but it's up to us to live in a way that unleashes it in our life and situations.

And yet it's possible to be an active participant in the church or call yourself a Christian and not live as an overcomer. God doesn't force His overcoming power or His strength on us. He has given each of us free will. That's why studying these seven churches and Jesus' messages to them is so important. Their lessons can help us in overcoming our own difficulties and wrongly placed desires.

EXPERIENTIAL REALITY

We all know it's possible for a couple to be married and yet not be happily married. In other words, their legal status isn't equal to their present experience. A marriage license declares one thing is true, but their reality says something else entirely. Similarly, when John says we have overcome, he's referring to our legal status under divine law. Christ has made every believer an overcomer legally, but that doesn't mean that's what we're experiencing personally. If a person is unhappy and married, that doesn't make them unmarried. It just makes them miserable while married. Likewise, if a person is a believer but living a defeated life, that doesn't make them not a Christian. It just makes them a defeated Christian.

So even though God has given you legal status in the heavenlies, your experiential reality might not line up accordingly. But the goal of spiritual growth—and our learning what we can in studying the seven churches Jesus addresses in Revelation—is making our legal status our experiential reality. To overcome experientially requires working out the power of God in our lives so that we experience it and the freedom it provides. To overcome means to overrule a sin or even an illegitimate set of circumstances.

And like the Supreme Court can overrule a lower court's judgment or a replay official can overrule a referee's call on the field, there is Someone who can overrule whatever is ruling you illegitimately. God has the final, overruling power. But it's up to you to tap into His power in order to live as an overcomer. So many believers have a legal relationship with God through salvation but fail to access His overarching power through an abiding relationship aligned under His rule. Thus, they live defeated by sin and circumstances.

The Bible makes it clear that to be an overcomer, a link must be made between your state and your standing, your position and your practice. What is legally true for you spiritually must also be what you experience relationally.

An example of such a gap is the difference between the Emancipation Proclamation and Juneteenth. Two and a half years passed between the legal issuance of the proclamation and the slaves in the Southwest states finally learning they were free. Even though they were legally free, they weren't literally free because the information regarding their freedom had not yet reached them. They couldn't act on the truth of that freedom.

The tragedy of Juneteenth, though, is that many people remained slaves even when the legal became literal for them, when they knew they were free. They were so used to slavery that they were afraid to exercise their freedom. This may seem remarkable to us now, but the same holds true for how many people view their sins, circumstances, or unhealthy relationships. They stay bound by them simply because the idea of freedom frightens them. How they live legally is not how they live experientially.

SEEING JESUS AS HE REALLY IS

To live as an overcomer, you need to seek God's power and strength, relying on His grace to transform you and help you find the courage to pursue true spiritual and emotional freedom. You need to renew your mind with the truth of God's Word, allowing it to shape your thoughts and attitudes, overcoming negative thought patterns and the lies of the enemy that hold you back. You also need to follow God's will for your life in a way that honors Him and His kingdom agenda.

But to do all that, you also need to see Jesus for who He truly is. You need to see Him the way John saw Him. This Jesus in the book of Revelation isn't the One we tack onto Sunday school flannel boards or hang nice pictures of on the walls of our churches. No, this Jesus is on fire.

John writes in Revelation 1:13-17:

> I saw one like a son of man, clothed in a robe reaching to the feet, and girded across His chest with a golden sash. His head and His hair were white like white wool, like snow; and His eyes were like a flame of fire. His feet were like burnished bronze, when it has been made to glow in a furnace, and His voice was like the sound of many waters. In His right hand He held seven stars, and out of

His mouth came a sharp two-edged sword; and His face was like the sun shining in its strength. When I saw Him, I fell at His feet like a dead man.

This description of Jesus portrays Him as a powerful and majestic figure, radiating divine glory and kingdom authority. His posture and attributes indicate great wisdom, strength, and stability. John became so overwhelmed by this triumphant and exalted Lord that all he could do was fall at His feet.

So this is not the sissified Jesus so many shrug Him off as these days. Rather, this is King Jesus who rules over all. This is the Jesus who "disarmed the rulers and authorities, [making] a public display of them, having triumphed over them through Him" (Colossians 2:15). Jesus stripped Satan and his minions of all authority when He disarmed them at the cross and even led a victory parade in the spiritual realm. Jesus didn't come to play; He secured our victory in His own.

That's why time and time again Scripture tells us we can overcome through Christ's overcoming power. We read this in multiple places, but here are three:

In all these things we overwhelmingly conquer through Him who loved us (Romans 8:37).

These things I have spoken to you, so that in Me you may have peace. In the world you have tribulation, but take courage; I have overcome the world (John 16:33).

God demonstrates His own love toward us, in that while we were yet sinners, Christ died for us...For if while we were enemies we were reconciled to God through the death of His Son, much more, having been reconciled, we shall be saved by His life (Romans 5:8-10).

Your ability to overcome is rooted and grounded in your relationship with Jesus Christ and His liberating power. On the cross, Jesus lifted the sins of the whole world and placed them on Himself. He took on the sin, pain, deceit, and destruction of it all and carried the burden.

Now, if a weight lifter can lift 700 pounds, you don't expect he'll have a problem lifting 200 pounds. Similarly, since Jesus took on the sins of the entire world on the cross, He won't have any problem helping you overcome whatever you're facing. No problem is too big for Jesus Christ. No addiction is too dug in that Jesus can't set you free. No circumstance or relationship is too far gone that He can't redeem it. He's already handled the whole world's sin and its accompanying circumstances.

Whatever you're facing may seem big to you, but know that it is not too big for Jesus. He can handle it. It's just that you may need to adjust which Jesus you're looking to for help. Are you looking to the Jesus the apostle John saw and wrote about in the book of Revelation? Are you looking to the Jesus who conquered Satan on the cross? Or are you looking to the Jesus our culture has dumbed down and gentled to fit inside a box of its own choosing?

If your view of Jesus is the correct view, then you'll know He can handle anything you're facing—plus a whole lot more. And when you tap into the power of the all-powerful One by viewing Jesus as who He truly is, you'll be able to do what John reveals he saw in a vision: "[The brethren] overcame [the accuser] because of the blood of the Lamb and because of the word of their testimony, and they did not love their life even when faced with death" (Revelation 12:11).

This one verse—as I'll show you next—can shift how you relate to Jesus. And when you do that, He shifts how He relates to you. By aligning yourself underneath Him, you access His care, covering, and power.

PREVAILING OVER THE ENEMY

The brethren John writes about in Revelation 12:11 prevailed over the enemy because of three actions they had in place, and we need to do the same three things.

1. Identify with Christ in Faith

When the people personally and publicly identified with Christ, they prevailed. See, God will often place victory in your reach, just not in your hand. Living as an overcomer is in your reach. You can have that life whenever you want. But you need to exercise faith in Christ in order to get it in your hand.

Now, talking about faith is not exercising faith. Praying about faith is good, but it's not exercising faith. Going to church is great, but it's not exercising faith either. To exercise faith in such a way that enables you to grab what God has to give requires identifying with Jesus Christ publicly through your walk and your talk, your life and your lips, your movement and your mouth. It's about your commitment and your confession.

In Galatians 2:20, Paul summarizes what this means not just for him but for all of us: "I have been crucified with Christ; and it is no longer I who live, but Christ lives in me; and the life which I now live in the flesh I live by faith in the Son of God, who loved me and gave Himself up for me." To identify with Jesus Christ means that He is your current point of reference. If what Jesus did two thousand years ago is just a historical event for you, you will never benefit from His power, as you have the potential to do.

The reality of what Jesus accomplished on the cross is a present-day reality. The power He exhibited on the cross is a present-day power. When He said even before His death and rise, "All authority has been given to Me in heaven and on earth" (Matthew 28:18), He wasn't talking about only a specific point in time. The translation of His statement is simply, "I'm in charge now!" Jesus did not come to take sides. He came to take over. He calls the shots. Thus, if you're not allowing Him to call the shots in your life—meaning you're making choices outside of His will and out from under His rule—you will not have access to His power and authority to overcome.

To identify with Jesus, then, is to identify with the power He displayed and the victory He secured on the cross.

2. Testify of Christ and His Lordship Publicly

We also see that the people overcame through the "word of their testimony." They were bold enough to speak up. If you live as a spiritual secret-agent, CIA representative, you can't expect Christ's power to be accessible to you. You can forget about overcoming if you're too embarrassed to be associated with Jesus.

In Matthew 10:33 Jesus says, "Whoever denies Me before men, I will also deny him before My Father who is in heaven." So if you don't want to be associated with Jesus publicly, if you're content with only a private meeting among saints on Sundays, then you have willingly given up Christ's power to overcome. Jesus is the all-powerful God. He decides whom He helps and when, and in part His decision rests in your relationship and public acknowledgment of Him.

Philippians 2:10 speaks of this testimony: "At the name of Jesus every knee will bow, of those who are in heaven and on earth and under the earth." God receives glory when Jesus is proclaimed publicly.

Confessing Jesus publicly can to some degree be compared to a married person wearing a wedding ring. That ring is there to publicly declare that they have a legal and binding relationship with someone else. Now, you can be married and choose not to wear a wedding ring, if that's the only indication, so no one will know you're married, but I doubt your spouse will smile on that choice.

Lots of people who have married into the family of God as the bride of Jesus Christ don't want to wear His ring. They don't want other people to know they're bound to Jesus in a covenantal relationship.

And when it's not "safe" for them to be associated with Him, they say—like Peter did—"I don't know the man." Because of this choice, however, in Matthew 10:33 Jesus makes it clear that when they call on Him to act as Mediator between them and God the Father, He will deny that He knows them. As long as a Christian is a secret-agent saint, they won't be accessing or maximizing both the kingdom power and authority that is rightfully theirs through the Lordship of Jesus Christ.

Jesus declares that a person's willingness to confess Him becomes the marker of their seriousness about Him. This is much more than simply believing in God. After all, Satan believes in God. Alignment under the Lordship of Christ—putting Him in first place—involves publicly declaring and demonstrating an association with Him in both words and actions.

The question stands: If you were accused of being a Christian, would there be enough evidence to convict you, or would you be found innocent of all charges? Again, Jesus makes a clear tie between His followers' public acknowledgment and confession of Him before men and His confession of us before the Father.

Now, keep in mind, Jesus doesn't say, "If you confess My Father before men, then I will confess you before Him." That's because it's easy for anyone to say they believe in God, to at least confess He exists. And people pour so many variant definitions into that one word that when it comes down to it, just saying "God" doesn't mean a whole lot anymore.

When you publicly confess Jesus Christ, however, everyone knows who you're talking about. The name Jesus is ultra specific. You're saying you believe in Him for eternal salvation, and you confess Him publicly for deliverance in history. Both His investment and His involvement in your life hinges on your public declaration through both your words and actions that He is Lord. As Paul boldly urged his protégé Timothy, "Do not be ashamed of the testimony of our Lord" (2 Timothy 1:8).

If for no other practical reason than accessing the power of deliverance on earth, you must establish and declare Jesus Christ as Lord in your life and over your world. You must open your mouth publicly and let others know through what you say—as well as what you do—that He is your Lord and Master, that you are not ashamed to be associated with Him and to live under Him. He is seated at the right hand of God in the heavenlies, as are you through His redemption on the cross. So access His power and authority through a public declaration of His Lordship in your life.

Furthermore, Jesus' blood has established the new covenant under which you are to align your life and world in order to receive its full covenantal covering and protection (Romans 12:11). You've probably heard someone say, "I plead the blood." They're talking about the blood of the covenant. The way you plead the blood of the covenant, however, is not by saying some supposedly magical words. You plead the blood of the covenant by being under the terms of the covenant—by making Jesus Christ Lord of your life and ruler of your world.

In Old Testament times, the Israelites couldn't just say, "I plead the blood." They had to place the blood of a slain animal on their doorposts in order to plead it. They had to align themselves within the protective confines of the walls that were connected to the bloodstained doors. Likewise, today there must be covenantal alignment under the Lordship and rulership of Jesus Christ in order to experience His kingdom power, authority, provision, and covering of an overcomer.

We read about this new covenant in these three places in the book of Hebrews:

> Now He has obtained a more excellent ministry, by as much as He is also the mediator of a better covenant, which has been enacted on better promises (Hebrews 8:6).

> He is the mediator of a new covenant, so that, since a death has taken place for the redemption of the transgressions that were committed under the first covenant, those who have been called may receive the promise of the eternal inheritance (Hebrews 9:15).

> And to Jesus, the mediator of a new covenant, and to the sprinkled blood, which speaks better than the blood of Abel (Hebrews 12:24).

Jesus Christ is the Lord of the new covenant, the unique one-of-a-kind Mediator between heaven and earth (1 Timothy 2:5).

I have a master key to the church building where I pastor. A staff person who works here may have a key to their own office, or even to the section of the building their office is in, but they're limited in which doors they can open throughout the facility. But because I have a master key that works in any lock, I can go anywhere I want.

Too many of us aren't getting everywhere we need to go because we don't have the *Master* key. We go to church, hear a sermon, and receive a truth, giving us a key for a certain room in our Christian lives, but the key to the Christian life as a whole is making Jesus Christ our Lord and Master. The ability to live victoriously and advance God's kingdom agenda on earth—in our churches, in our communities, and around the world—comes through this unique Master key called the Lordship of Christ.

And only as the Lordship of Jesus Christ is reflected through His people individually and corporately will the world experience the rule of God as the Creator intended it to be. Only as the Lordship of Jesus Christ is reflected through your life individually will you tap into the overcoming power and authority that is His to supply.*

---

* The content in this chapter beginning with the paragraph "Confessing Jesus publicly" is adapted with permission from Tony Evans, *The Kingdom Agenda* (Chicago, IL: Moody Publishers, 2013).

3. Be Willing to Sacrifice All for Christ

The third thing Romans 12:11 reveals we must do to overcome is seek a relationship with Jesus that transcends even death—and in more than one kind of death. The verse says, "They did not love their life even when faced with death." Many of the early church believers had to make this third aspect real in their lives physically. But we're also called to a daily death. This is what Paul was talking about when he said he "died daily" (1 Corinthians 15:31). And it's what Jesus meant in Luke 9:23 when He said, "If anyone wishes to come after Me, he must deny himself, and take up his cross daily and follow Me." These believers' commitment to Christ, then, was so strong that they were willing to sacrifice their own wants and desires as well as their lives in order to demonstrate it.

In our culture today, our physical lives aren't often threatened for following Jesus, but the principle remains true. We should be willing to sacrifice our wants and desires to demonstrate our commitment to Christ, at a minimum. In doing so, we will discover the overcoming power of His relationship with us.

Jesus is to be the sum total of your existence, and when you view Him as your Source and sole provider for all things—not just material needs, but also your emotional, spiritual, and any other needs—then making these commitments to Him will come easy. Living as an overcomer is all about a close and abiding relationship with Jesus Christ. And we'll discover more about this in Part Two of this book, diving more deeply into studying the seven churches Jesus addresses in the book of Revelation.

JESUS' MESSAGES TO THE SEVEN CHURCHES

Jesus thought it was important for Him to tell the seven churches in what was then Asia Minor what they needed to know specific to their current situation, both the good and the bad. But He's talking to us too. We may live and worship in America in the twenty-first century, but that doesn't mean the truths and warnings, the promises and rewards we see in Revelation chapters 2 and 3 aren't relevant for us today. They most certainly are.

Let's start with the church in Ephesus and go all the way through to the church in Laodicea—the group about which Jesus seems to have had the most concern.

2

PUTTING GOD
IN FIRST PLACE

You've seen the swoosh. It's everywhere. And it often comes attached to the words *Just Do It*. The Nike swoosh represents strength, power, conquering, and victory. But did you know the word *nike* comes from the Greek word for overcomer? It's the word we examined in our opening chapter: *nikeo*. Nike is the English cognate of this Greek term. It borrows from the Greek goddess of victory in Greek mythology.

God wants you to win. He wants you to live with strength, power, and an ability to conquer whatever life throws at you. The word *nikeo* assumes life will do that, that there's something or someone seeking to defeat you, oppress you, or keep you living as a victim. And there usually is.

But we also need to ensure we have our priorities straight, and that's the theme of Jesus' message to the first church we come to—Ephesus.

WHAT EPHESUS WAS LIKE

To appreciate and understand Ephesus, picture New York City. I love that city, so I have no problem visualizing what Ephesus may have been like back in their day.

Ephesus was the premiere city in Asia Minor, now known as Turkey. It was the region's center of commerce, culture, fashion, and civic focus. If you wanted to vacation, you'd go to Ephesus. It was a tourist hub. And it was an economic boomtown. In some ways it was also like New York's Wall Street. Because of its strategic location, Ephesus was where significant financial matters were addressed.

To sum it up, Ephesus had it going on!

It also served as a host for an enormous amount of idolatry. The temple of Diana, also known as the Temple of Artemis or the Artemisium, served as a major idolatrous attraction, drawing people from all over that part of the world with different backgrounds, cultures, and even ideologies.

Although many gods and idols were sought out in Ephesus in order to offer sacrifices and worship, Diana drew the highest bidding and most attention. She was the goddess of fertility, the twin sibling of Apollo, and represented health, wealth, and hunting. Her temple was enormous in size, roughly double the dimensions of most other temples. It was so huge, in fact, that it was named one of the seven ancient wonders of the world.

Ephesus had a lot to offer its citizens. And what's more, in the midst of this bustling, wealthy, and idolatrous metropolis, the apostle Paul had planted a church—the church to whom he wrote a letter that became the book of Ephesians in the Bible.

The story of the church's start-up is told in Acts 19. In a city full of sorcery, witchcraft, and all manner of idolatry, people were saved because of the teaching being done in and through this church. When you read Acts 19, you'll no doubt pick up on this brand-new church's energy and excitement as well as the challenges they faced.

They made a lot of positive impact with that excitement and dedication, but they somehow got off track along the way. That's where they are when they show up in the book of Revelation.

JESUS' MESSAGE BEGINS

Jesus' message to the church in Ephesus starts out strong. It begins with an introduction and then a commendation before it gets into their problem.

John records what Jesus wants the angel of the church of Ephesus to say:

> The One who holds the seven stars in His right hand, the
> One who walks among the seven golden lampstands, says
> this: "I know your deeds and your toil and perseverance,
> and that you cannot tolerate evil men, and you put to the
> test those who call themselves apostles, and they are not,
> and you found them to be false; and you have perseverance
> and have endured for My name's sake, and have not grown
> weary" (Revelation 2:1-3).

Jesus starts with wanting the church to know He knows what He's talking about. He knows who they are. He knows where they came from. He knows where they've been and even what they're thinking. He doesn't want any hesitation concerning their hearing from Him in this way, so He sets the stage with who He truly is and what He knows. A hesitant hearer can lead to a lack of response to what is said, so He first establishes His command. Not only can He hold seven stars in His hand and walk among seven lampstands, but He also sees everything.

Then He shifts to a compliment. He congratulates the church by telling them He's aware of their good deeds. He's aware of their commitment. He's aware that they are a serving church. He knows their programs, ministries, outreaches, and preaching. He even knows about their Scripture study classes and their "breaking free" support groups. He knows they seek to do all they do with excellence and proficiency. The church in Ephesus truly exists as a model serving church, full of active members.

In fact, they serve so much that He reveals they do it even to the point of personal exhaustion. That's what the word *toil* means. He commends them for both toiling and persevering in all they do. They labor. They sweat. They put in the overtime necessary to do the job of serving others well. This church contains individuals who don't know the word *quit*. If they lived today, they would certainly be a megachurch simply due to their reputation. Their social media videos would have millions of views because the message they proclaim is inspiring and motivational. They live what they teach. And when the going gets tough, they don't toss in any towels. This is a steadfast church where serving is the norm.

Then He acknowledges that He's well aware of this church and its representatives' longevity. He's well aware that they have endured for His name's sake. They don't tolerate evil men. They are orthodox in both theology and doctrine. They are a Scripture-teaching, Scripture-believing, Scripture-quoting, and Scripture-doting church. They measure all things by the standard of the truth of God's Word. This is a church to get excited about!

Yet despite all of this—the serving, sacrificing, steadfastness, separation from the world, and even suffering for their faith—this commendation is quickly followed by a criticism. Apparently, they got it all right except for one key thing, and that one key thing is massive.

WHAT ABOUT YOUR FIRST LOVE?

"But I have this against you," the angel continues, "that you have left your first love" (verse 4). Let that sink in. Talk about a wake-up twist to the plotline. This Scripture-based church with a litany of great things attached to their name and reputation is called out publicly for missing *one* thing. You would think they were about to be applauded and highlighted as a model for the other six churches. You would think that all they were doing right was about to become a standard for the others to aim toward. You would think they would at least get a pass based on all of the praise Jesus just gave them. But no, His message didn't go that way at all. Because though Jesus had been their first love, their first priority, He no longer was. And He knew it.

This teaches us that, evidently, today you can be a serving church, or even a serving Christian, and still wildly miss the mark. You can be a sacrificing church, or a sacrificing Christian, and get off track. You can be a steadfast church, or a steadfast Christian, while falling far short of God's goal. You can be a church separated from the world, or a Christian separated from the world, and be far from Christ in your heart. You can be a suffering church, or a suffering Christian, and have left your first love.

In short, you can do everything right while still functioning in a very wrong relational style.

If you and I are to daily live as overcomers, we must pay attention to the message given to this nearly model church in Ephesus. This miss of theirs is subtle, and that's why it can easily be missed in our own lives. God must not only be loved by us; He must be loved *first*. The issue with Ephesus wasn't that they no longer loved God; it was that they no longer loved Him first. He was no longer their relational and heart's priority.

God cannot lie or sin, but there's another thing He can't do. He can't be in second position or even lower than that in the lives of any of His followers. The Bible regularly tells us about His rightful jealousy (Exodus 20:5; 34:14; Deuteronomy 4:24; 32:16; Joshua 24:19; Psalm 79:5; 2 Corinthians 11:2). This jealousy is rooted in God's character and commitment to us, and because of who He is, He both demands and deserves first priority in our lives.

Are you old enough to remember when cars had no seat belts or center consoles in their front seats? I am, and I'll tell you something interesting about what that revealed. If one person in a couple sat way over on the opposite end of the front seat from the driver, next to the window, that indicated a possible rift in their relationship. Now, that wasn't because the driver had moved. It was because the passenger had moved.

Similarly, if you and Jesus aren't as close as you used to be, or not close at all, it's not because He's moved. It's because you've scooted away from Him. But God created and saved you for a love relationship with Him, not to perform ritualistic duties. Any AI or cyborg could have been created to perform duties. God desires that you love Him and that your actions reflect, or stem from, a heart of loving Him as your first priority.

To love is to decide to compassionately pursue the well-being of another. To love God first is to passionately pursue His pleasure, to pursue that which brings Him glory and good. To love God first doesn't merely mean serving Him or singing about Him. Nor does it merely mean telling Him you love Him in your prayers. Love is always reflected in actions that originate from the heart.

Suppose a husband told his wife he loved her and valued her but that she couldn't be the first priority in his life. What if he told her he would slide her in when he could. He would still provide an income for their family, and he wouldn't cheat on her, but he would get around to spending time with her only when he had some hours or energy to spare. Do you think the wife would be satisfied with that kind of "love"? Neither do I.

But that's what we often do with God yet expect Him to be delighted with us. We tell Him we love Him, but by our actions, we also tell Him that He can't be first for us. Sure, we'll still work and serve. We'll still attend church and say prayers. But when it comes to spending time together and knowing and experiencing each other, God will have to wait until we have time or energy to spare.

This is not placing God first. This is not making Him our priority.

FIRST FRUITS

The book of Proverbs emphasizes God's first place in our lives with regard to our material goods. It says, "Honor the LORD from your wealth and from the first of all your produce" (3:9). Many people don't readily see how "first fruits" in an agrarian culture applies to us today, but the principle tied to it transcends time.

The issue of first fruits involves dedicating your best and your first to God. It involves honoring Him with what we call a "tithe" (Deuteronomy 26:10-13). People in biblical times measured their giving according to the produce they received. If it was from ten acres of farmland, they dedicated the first acre's produce to God. Or if it was a flock of lambs, they honored God by giving the first male of the flock. In giving God the first and the best of what they relied on for their personal sustenance and survival, they were worshiping Him as their ultimate Source (Deuteronomy 14:26).

While today we aren't farmers bringing God our tithe in the form of physical produce, we know that produce was a form of income in biblical culture. So it's easy to translate the call to tithe to a monetary gift today. Both honor God.

The New Testament designates that our first and best gift is to be given on the first day of the week (1 Corinthians 16:2). This is where we get the correlation of giving to God during Sunday worship services. I understand that not everyone is paid weekly and that giving online or through other forms can and does honor God as much as giving each Sunday, but the principle of putting God first is what matters most.

WHY "FIRST" MATTERS

This message of putting God first shows up all throughout the Bible. Deuteronomy 6:5 says, "You shall love the LORD your God with all your heart and with all your soul and with all your might." *All* cannot mean second place. *All* can only mean first place.

One of my favorite passages sums it up best: "Seek first [God's] kingdom and His righteousness, and all these things will be added to you" (Matthew 6:33). If you're serving God yet not from a position of putting Him first, you're really putting yourself first. You're merely fulfilling a duty because you think there's a reward or a prize for you up ahead. The church in Ephesus did a lot for God, but it had all shifted into being done from a heart of duty, not of love. Their duty had trumped their devotion. Their regulations about God ruined their relationship with Him. As a result, they had left their first love.

In baseball, if you miss first base, you'll never score. It doesn't matter if you hit a home run. It doesn't matter if you run as fast as you can. It doesn't even matter if you touch second base, third base, and even home plate. If you don't touch first base first, you don't score.

Far too many believers are running as fast as they can and swinging for the fences as hard as they can, all the while missing what matters most. They're missing the heartfelt devotion to Jesus Christ that puts Him first. And when Jesus is no longer first, then whatever has replaced Him, even if it's your own self-absorption, is an idol. As far as how God views your duty to Him, you have moved down the street from the church house and entered the temple of Artemis with everyone else. Whatever is first in your heart becomes your god.

That's not to say you don't love God. That's not to say you don't know Jesus personally. But when you've let anything usurp the Lord's rightful place in your thoughts, words, emotions, or actions, *that* has become first in your life. God is no longer your first priority.

PERFORMANCE OVER RELATIONSHIP

One way to tell when first love within you has turned to second love—or worse—is noticing that performance for God has become an end in itself. If your checklist garners more focus than checking in with God, you have lost your first love.

Whenever I preach simply to preach rather than preaching out of a heartfelt love for and devotion to the Lord, I have left my first love. Whenever you spend time in daily devotions just to cross it off your list, you have left your first love. God knows everything, and He especially knows when we're pursuing a performance rather than cultivating a relationship.

In the Christian walk, it's possible to go through a program and a process all the while missing the person of Christ. It's possible to cross off a long list of spiritual duties, all the while missing the cross. This is because if a relationship is based on a list, there's a problem in that relationship. In fact, this devolves into living the Christian life by law rather than by grace (Galatians 5:4).

Unfortunately, far too many believers live this way. They assume that to be a good Christian they need to do this, that, and the other, all the while avoiding this, that, and the other. When they have the items on their list completely checked off, they think the Lord must be happy with them.

This Bible story about sisters Martha and Mary sheds light on the problem (Luke 10:38-42). Martha is busy in the kitchen cooking up a full meal for Jesus while Mary is sitting at His feet, enjoying an intimate relationship with Him. So upset with Mary that she doesn't even call her into the kitchen herself, Martha comes out and complains to Jesus. She wants to know why He doesn't tell her sister to help make the meal.

Do you recall what Jesus says in response? We read it in verses 41 and 42: "Martha, Martha, you are worried and bothered about so many things; but only one thing is necessary, for Mary has chosen the good part, which shall not be taken away from her." Jesus plainly tells Martha He won't send Mary into the kitchen to cook. (Then He would have two "Marthas" to deal with.) Only one thing is necessary, He tells her—being with Him. In other words, a casserole in the oven would do if it would free up Martha to come spend time with Him as well.

A lot of us keep a list of what good we're doing for God but we have a much shorter list for how we're deepening our relationship with Him. Whenever devotion to a relationship fades, the relationship is in trouble. God doesn't just want your programming and deeds; He wants your passion. He wants the fire.

WHAT HAPPENED TO THE FIRE?

How many couples have said the fire in their relationship is no longer there? They've drifted apart. But for the fire in a fireplace or firepit to stay hot, there must be an ongoing, intimate connection between the logs. Once that connection disappears, so does the fire. It doesn't matter if you have a million matches at that point. Each one may light a fire, but the flame will soon disappear. To keep a fire burning, the logs must be connected—intimately. They keep each other hot.

This is similar to how many people approach their relationship with God. They seek being lit with only a match—again and again. Maybe that's by coming to church and singing worship songs, but by the time they hit the parking lot, the fire is gone. Their spiritual vitality has vanished because what started as a relationship with God has devolved into a ritual. What started as intimacy drifted into activity. They lost their fire. They left their first love.

What Jesus is saying to the Christians at Ephesus—and subsequently to each one of us who has an ear to hear—is that duty is never to replace devotion if we want to be an overcomer. Rather, devotion is to transform duty into something desirable, done out of a heart of love and generated by a relationship rooted in the priority of intimacy.

This reminds me of the story about a guy playing golf when a funeral procession passes by the course he's on. He drops his club. He kneels. He bows his head. All to pay homage to the deceased. When the funeral procession comes to an end, he stands to play golf again.

The caddy with him remarks, "Wow, that was really respectful. What made you do all of that?"

"Well, I was married to her for 35 years, so it seemed right."

The man's actions looked respectful, but when you know the context for them, you see they were anything but respectful. In fact, it would be more than a little dismissive for any husband to miss his wife's funeral in order to play golf.

Many people see Christians' actions and think they're all about God. But only God knows your whole story. He knows your heart. He knows whether or not you find time for Him even though you have a lot of other things going on. He knows whether you check in to subscription TV before you ever check in with Him. He knows if you're crossing items off your list in hopes of a reward or with a desire to avoid negative consequences in your life. And He knows that even though you can do an awful lot of good things for Him, if you don't put Him first, they're just *good things*. They're not *good works*.

But God created you for and calls you to good works (Ephesians 2:10). And those good works arise from within your heart, carried out of a spirit of love that seeks to glorify God and bring others good.

STEPS IN THE RIGHT DIRECTION

First has everything to do with priority. God wants to be relationally prioritized, not just programmed into your life. He wants to make sure you don't allow the rituals of religion to merely soothe you like when babies suck on a pacifier, giving them the impression of sustenance when none is there. It's no surprise, then, that Jesus starts His messages to the seven churches with the problem of not putting Him first. After all, if you miss that, nothing else matters. God must be first.

If like the church in Ephesus, you have failed to keep God first in your heart and in your life, notice verse 5 in Revelation 2. It gives you three steps to get back in alignment with Him—and it tells you what will happen if you don't take them: "Remember from where you have fallen, and repent and do the deeds you did at first; or else I am coming to you and will remove your lampstand out of its place—unless you repent."

Let's look at these three steps—and then one more to take as well.

1. Remember What It Was Like Before

God makes the start of the solution simple and straightforward. If He's no longer the priority love in your life, remember when He was. Remember when He was all you had and when He mattered most. Remember that when you didn't know how you were going to make it—recover from that illness or financial difficulty, find a spouse, get the job you need, leave a toxic relationship, or whatever it was—you looked to Him first.

Or remember when you were first saved and He was always first on your mind. You knew He had your back because He also had your heart. When you remember how things were, you'll recognize how to get back to that.

2. Repent of Your Sin

Second, we must repent. Now, there's only one thing a person repents of in the Bible, and that's sin. So that means leaving your first love is considered a sin. It's not just a mistake. It's not just a bad habit. It's not an "oops." When your relationship with God is relegated to second place or even less than that, you're living in sin.

God isn't asking the church in Ephesus to listen to a motivational video on prioritizing their lives. He's telling them to repent from their sin. This isn't a time-management issue. It's not a scheduling issue. It's a sin issue. And the only way to exit a lifestyle of sin is through heartfelt repentance. Repentance involves a change of mind in order to reverse a direction.

3. Repeat What You Did at the Start

Then the church is told to "repeat" what they did at the start. They're called to "do the deeds you did at first." That means repeating what they once were all about—prioritizing God in first place. To apply this principle in your own life, look closely at when God *was* first. What did you do without even thinking twice? How did you talk to God then? Did you make time for reading and studying His Word? To return to the place of prioritizing Jesus, you'll need to return to what you did when He was your first priority.

John 14:21 sums up this connection between love and action: "He who has My commandments and keeps them is the one who loves Me; and he who loves Me will be loved by My Father, and I will love him and will disclose Myself to him." When you return to God not only with all your heart, mind, and soul but with all your actions, He reveals Himself to you like never before. He discloses Himself to you.

Sadly, the reason so many people aren't experiencing the overcoming power of God is that He doesn't feel free to disclose Himself. God will not disclose Himself to someone who puts Him second. Why should He unveil His plan for your life if He knows you're just going to replace Him with something or someone else? That's why it's so important to put God first. You've got to go against your inclinations, laziness, or even your schedule.

When you do begin to return God to first place in your life, part of His overcoming power is made known to you as He discloses His wisdom, will, and strength to you. You will be given the gift of overcoming. We read about this gift in the second part of Revelation 2:7: "To him who overcomes, I will grant to eat of the tree of life which is in the Paradise of God."

Only the overcomers are granted this gift. Only those who overcome will get to eat of the tree of life in the paradise of God. Only those who overcome gain access to the future reward of this special interaction and access in heaven. Only overcomers gain the opportunity to partake of this special food from this unique tree. This intimacy comes by invitation. It's a future intimacy reserved for those who place a high value on intimacy with God while on earth.

But you also get the overcoming power of God's disclosing Himself to you in the present. While a future reward is special, it doesn't necessarily help you in the here and now. So this reward comes both in the present as well. As God discloses Himself to you here on earth, you'll discover what you are to do, where you are to go, what purpose He has for you, what brings you your greatest joy, how to have healthy relationships, and so much more. You'll discover the wisdom He has available to you when you draw near to Him in a relationship rooted and grounded in pure love.

Here, then, is a fourth step important for you to take.

4. Embrace the Reward of Truly Knowing God

Knowing God is a reward all unto itself. But knowing God is very different from knowing about God. When I was in seminary and studying the Bible in classes day and night, I actually grew more distant from God. Even though I was in the Word so regularly, I'd made the study of the Word my goal rather than knowing the Author of the Word. As a result, I got *A*s in my classes but an *F* in my relationship with God.

Years later, as I worked on my study Bible and commentary, I had matured to the point where I knew not to do that again. I paced my study so that it would not become a goal in and of itself. I studied the Scriptures and then wrote much of the commentary as part of my daily devotional time in God's Word. Because I was able to spread this work out over many years, I never lost touch with the Author while learning more about what He wrote. In fact, my relationship with Him deepened as I experienced and interacted with His living Word on such a regular, in-depth level. He revealed Himself to me in fresh and new ways.

What I didn't know was that He was preparing me to walk through the deepest valley of my life. Not long after I finished the study Bible and commentary project, I lost eight family members in a span of two years, including my beloved wife, my only sister, my older brother, and my father. God knew that in order to overcome in that season, I needed closeness with Him that didn't allow me to throw in the towel. Through those years of study and spending time with Him in His Word, He prepared me in a way that caused me to seek Him first—not the outcome nor the goal of the project itself.

When you truly know God—His thoughts, His heart, and His ways, whether through His Word or in prayer—you'll be able to overcome anything and everything you face. Why? Because you'll be close to the One who has already overcome it all (John 16:33), making Him more than worthy of first place in your life. In Him, you will have the peace, strength, and power you need to get through difficult days.

EXHIBITING STEADY FAITHFULNESS

THE CHURCH IN SMYRNA
(Revelation 2:8-11)

As Americans, you and I are living in the midst of a divided society with political chaos. The battle for power and control is part of our history, but now we have a front-row seat to its playing out once again before our very eyes.

One of the key strategies you'll notice when political parties seek to win an election is their targeting "undecided voters." Also known as "swing voters," they can literally swing an outcome one way or the other. That's why much if not most of the discourse surrounding policies and approaches to government concern the topics that most matter to them. And politicians know better than to try to persuade a staunch Democrat to vote Republican or a staunch Republican to vote Democrat. Rarely do lifelong single-party voters—or even generational party voters—change alignments. So because they can make or break an entire campaign, it's these voters who get the focus.

While we can easily comprehend this reality and recognize it in our societal structure and discourse, we may not always realize how many "undecided Christians" God's got in His kingdom on earth. These are Christians who lay claim to Him by name as long as everything in their lives is going well. But when the going gets tough, they aren't really sure where they stand. In fact, with their feet firmly planted in midair because their stand is both ambivalent and ambiguous, they wind up looking like many politicians.

God has a major issue when it comes to part-time Christians who refuse to live as full-time saints. He doesn't see eye to eye with those who come to Him for blessings but kick Him to the curb when struggles surface. These individuals tend to want the benefits of heaven, but they don't want to bother with the spiritual work that brings heaven's benefits to bear on earth.

The apostle John writes to the second church about this very issue—faithfulness rather than vulnerability to the winds and whims of change.

JESUS IS THE ONE

This second church was located in Smyrna, roughly 35 miles north of our previous church, Ephesus. Smyrna was a well-known seaport town, and its inhabitants were very well off and somewhat prestigious. They also had buildings erected in the form of a crown. Why? Because it was one of the cities in Asia that focused on emperor worship. (More about that shortly.)

Smyrna was also a place where resident Christians were undergoing a great deal of tribulation and trial because they were true public kingdom disciples. They weren't secretive about their faith. And because of the troubles they constantly faced, in His message through the angel Jesus introduces Himself in this manner: "The first and the last, who was dead, and has come to life" (Revelation 2:8).

In light of what He's about to say concerning their coming persecution, Jesus makes a point of letting them know He is the One who was dead but is now alive. He wants them to know that if anyone understands troubles and trials, it's Him. He knows continual faithfulness—the call He's about to make to them—is possible despite horrific circumstances.

He knows because He's done it. And that's the beautiful thing about Jesus Christ. He can relate to our troubles. He can relate to us as God in heaven, but He can also relate to us down here on earth. He went through pain and suffering, even to the point of death, and He remained obedient in it all. That's why He introduces Himself to the Smyrna church by identifying Himself as the One who died but was also raised. He wants to let them know that death does not have the last word. No amount of suffering has the last word.

Jesus wanted them and us to realize that overcoming means our problems are not the bottom line. Overcoming means what you see is not what you ultimately get. It means Calvary Friday is overruled by Resurrection Sunday. And whatever death you may be facing right now—the death of a relationship, your career, your financial well-being, your good health, or even a dream—Jesus wants you to know He has the final word on all of it. He has the final word because He *is* the first, and He *is* the last. He has died, but He has also risen.

The uniqueness of Christ should never go overlooked in our understanding of Scripture. His uniqueness is what makes Him powerful and able to help you overcome anything you face. The baby in the manger made His mother. The baby in the stable made the animals that surrounded Him there. The same person who got thirsty could also walk on water. The same person who got hungry could turn sardines and crackers into a Moby Dick sandwich. The same person who could die on a cross could rise again.

Jesus is the ascended Christ. And because of who He is and all He has overcome and can overcome, we are to look to Him in His current status, as the One in charge of all. This perspective alone will enable you to overcome what life throws at you.

JESUS UNDERSTANDS—AND SO CAN WE

Then Jesus wants them to know He understands their current circumstances: "I know your tribulation and your poverty (but you are rich), and the blasphemy by those who say they are Jews and are not, but are a synagogue of Satan" (Revelation 2:9).

Jesus isn't just making a kind remark. He knows the people in this church are truly in pain, and He's reminding them that He knows what they've gone through and are facing right then. Nothing has caught Him by surprise. Jesus never says "Oops" when it comes to running this world we live in. He is fully aware of all you go through because He is fully God. He is also fully aware of how what you go through makes you feel, because He was also fully a man.

If you feel like you can't keep up with emotional pressures, know that Jesus knows your pain. If you're having trouble paying your bills, know that Jesus knows your stress. If you're crying, know that He not only knows you're crying but knows how that feels. If your world has been shaken, know that Jesus is aware of that, too, not only because He's an omniscient God who transcends time and space, but because He lived a fully human life while on earth. In other words, Jesus is your Savior, but He's also your *compassionate* Savior.

So when He sends the individuals in the church in Smyrna His message, Jesus first wants them know that He feels what they feel. He offers the common ground of compassion before He talks about their future.

"DO NOT BE AFRAID"

Smyrna was a Roman colony where most of the people worshiped Caesar as their lord. In fact, Roman citizens were required to recognize Caesar as their god. But the Christians who lived in Smyrna had another point of view. They refused to worship Caesar and instead exalted Jesus Christ as Lord over all. This inevitably created a conflict with the Roman government. Thus, they were going through the pressure and oppression of not yielding to the governmental authority with regard to their claimed right of deity.

They were, in short, an enemy of the State and placed on a watch list. Their property was confiscated and they couldn't access the funds in their bank accounts. Jesus reveals this when He mentions they are rich, meaning spiritually, yet live in poverty.

Living in poverty can complicate a difficulty even more than the difficulty itself, primarily because people with money often use it to suppress or even hide how messed up they feel. You can spend money on entertainment. You can spend money on parties. You can spend money on retail therapy. You can spend money on any number of things to mask how you truly feel. But since the Christians in Smyrna lived in poverty, they were face-to-face with their pain. They were spiritually rich because of their commitment to Christ, but that commitment came with a hefty price tag.

Some of you may identify with what it means to suffer for your Christian beliefs. Maybe you've been discriminated against in your job. In America, we're getting to the place where if you publicly declare Jesus Christ as Lord anywhere at all, you could be setting yourself up for attack. That's why this message Paul sends to young Timothy rings truer each year: "Indeed, all who desire to live godly in Christ Jesus will be persecuted" (2 Timothy 3:12).

If you've never suffered rejection or loss because of your Christian faith, beliefs, and values, it may be a result of living according to your own rules, not God's. Scripture is clear that all who live as kingdom disciples under the Lordship of Jesus Christ will suffer persecution in some form or fashion. For example, Paul tells the Thessalonians in 1 Thessalonians 3:4, "When we were with you, we kept telling you in advance that we were going to suffer affliction; and so it came to pass."

One of the goals of the liberal secular agenda is to bankrupt the church by accusing it of discrimination. Many Christian business owners have come under increased scrutiny for their values. But when your ultimate allegiance is to Christ, not to secular concerns or even duly elected seats of government, facing societal challenges is part of the package.

That's what the believers in Smyrna faced. Underneath the sovereign hand of God, who allowed them to experience suffering and persecution, their faith was tested.

WHY WE'RE TESTED

God often allows this testing so we will come to know Him in a more personal way. Then He expects three things from us: that we extend our experience of His compassion and kindness to others, that we grow in our walk with Him, and that we work to increase our intimacy with Him.

1. Extending Compassion and Kindness to Others

Paul writes in 2 Corinthians 1:3-5:

> Blessed be the God and Father of our Lord Jesus Christ, the Father of mercies and God of all comfort, who comforts us in all our affliction so that we will be able to comfort those who are in any affliction with the comfort with which we ourselves are comforted by God. For just as the sufferings of Christ are ours in abundance, so also our comfort is abundant through Christ.

So one reason God lets His followers go through pain and troubles even when we're trying to please Him and publicly associate with Him is that He knows somebody down the line will need comfort too. He doesn't want us to just offer a prayer for someone in need; He wants us to demonstrate the love of Christ through compassion and kindness. Like Jesus did, He wants us to extend those to others where they are. In this way, we transfer the love of Jesus to whomever may need it most.

2. Growing in Our Walk with Christ

Another reason God allows believers who obediently follow Him to experience suffering is to help them grow. We read in James 1:2-4, "Consider it all joy, my brethren, when you encounter various trials, knowing that the testing of your faith produces endurance. And let endurance have its perfect result, so that you may be perfect and complete, lacking in nothing."

God allows various trials to enter our lives in order to take us to another level of spiritual growth. There is always purpose in your pain as a believer. If and when you seek to live publicly for Jesus and according to His will, you must trust His plan even when you don't understand His hand at work in your circumstances. God will allow people to come against you, reject you, scheme against you, politic against you, or dismiss you for His reasons and purposes. But He is about much more than what you can ever see on the surface or in the situation. God works behind the scenes to develop, strengthen, and guide you to His intended kingdom agenda for you.

3. Increasing Our Intimacy with Christ

God also allows us to be tested to deepen His reality in our lives—for us to have a more intimate relationship with Him. In Philippians 3:10, this is referred to as "the fellowship of His sufferings." Fellowship refers to increased intimacy. It means coming to know Jesus in such a way that He becomes real to you in your daily life. If you turn to Jesus only when you need an answer to a question or want a blessing or protection or bailout, that's not truly knowing Him and all He has to offer you.

God will also often allow difficulties to come into your days so that you become desperate enough to truly seek Him. He lets you feel what

He felt when He suffered on earth. He knows that when you do, you will snuggle up closer to Him. You will spend more time with Him in prayer. You will read more of His Word. You will come to know His heart.

God also knows if you respond to adversity with bitterness and blame, you will only prolong your suffering and perhaps even add to it. But if you respond spiritually, you'll grow closer to Him.

THE SMYRNA CHURCH RECEIVES TRUTH AND A WARNING

Once Jesus established the common ground of a shared understanding of suffering, and once He let the congregants at Smyrna know how much He cared for them and understood what they were going through, He moved into a deeper truth and warning. We read what He wants the angel to tell them next in verse 10: "Do not fear what you are about to suffer. Behold, the devil is about to cast some of you into prison, so that you will be tested, and you will have tribulation for ten days."

Jesus didn't mince words. After acknowledging their suffering, He let them know that they are about to suffer even more. He basically says, "You think it's been bad? You ain't seen nothin' yet!" That's why He encouraged them to not be afraid. It's easy to become afraid when you're hurting because of your faith. It's easy to be afraid when you're being oppressed or wounded. It's easy to be afraid when your present feels uncertain and your future seems dark. So Jesus reminds them to not be afraid as their troubles worsen. He tells them to not be afraid because He's got His hand on the clock. Only He will determine how long they will have to suffer.

Anyone who cooks uses a timer to tell them when their casserole or roast or lasagna is ready to come out of the oven, to let them know the food has cooked long enough. Were it to be taken out of the oven too soon, it would not be done. Were it to be taken out too late, it could be burned or even ruined.

God has a timer for the troubles we face. In the case of the believers in Smyrna, He told them it would be ten days. They were about to suffer ten days of difficulties, darkness, and despair. But He wanted them to know their agony would not go on without end. If they would just persevere, they would reach the other side of pain.

Most people don't realize Satan is on a leash. He's been given room to roam this earth and makes a mess based on mankind's rebellion and yielding to his authority, but ultimately, he's on a leash. He can go only so far and no further. God's sovereignty doesn't allow Satan to call the shots. Whatever he wants to do must first be filtered through God's sovereign plan.

That's why Jesus could confidently say the increased troubles the believers in Smyrna were about to face had a stopping point. The devil is God's devil, and He will use him as He wants. If you don't believe me, just ask the suffering man Job in the Old Testament. God tells the devil how far he can go and how long he can stay to cause trouble.

This is also why God was the one who told Moses when it was time to seek the release of the Israelite slaves in Egypt. God had established the time of their release. Pharaoh may have thought he was in control. He may have gotten the big head thinking he was calling the shots. But God was who determined when it was time for His people to be released.

The key principle to keep in mind as you follow Jesus Christ is His sovereignty. He is the self-sufficient, eternal One who determines the ultimate outcome. Staying close to Jesus gives you the strength to endure and the wisdom to learn while you're going through difficulties. What God desires is that you keep your eyes on Him during the troubles at hand.

BE FAITHFUL AS CHRIST IS FAITHFUL

Then in Revelation 2:10 Jesus goes on to say, "Be faithful until death, and I will give you the crown of life." He asked the believers in

Smyrna to be faithful until death, and He is asking the same of each one of us. Faithfulness means dependability regardless of circumstances.

Sometimes it's easy to be faithful to the Lord because life is going your way. But other times you truly want to bail. It becomes difficult to remain faithful when your days have become confusing and hard, especially when you're suffering for doing what's right. You start to ask where is the reward for following God.

Jesus knows those questions come up within, and that's why He made sure the believers in Smyrna heard about their reward for pressing through—the "crown of life." Keep in mind, He was speaking to people who lived in a city surrounded by mountains that resembled a crown. They knew what a crown meant. They knew a crown signified authority, power, rule, and recognition. Wearing a crown indicated a privileged position. Those who pushed through the pain of the coming ten excruciating days of suffering, even to the point of death, were about to get one of the greatest rewards of all: the crown of life, namely a higher ruling position with Christ.

With this revelation of a reward came a greater explanation of what Jesus meant by "He who has an ear, let him hear what the Spirit says to the churches. He who overcomes will not be hurt by the second death" (verse 11). The church members in Smyrna would have to overcome the temptation to abandon their faith during tough times. Jesus was asking them to overcome the temptation to walk away from God. If they did overcome that temptation, they would be rewarded by being protected from the hurt of the second death.

The second death refers to hell (Revelation 20:14-15). Scripture describes hell as a lake of fire. But since these believers were already Christians, it's curious that their reward would be to escape something they would have already escaped by being a Christian to begin with. That's why we need to dig deeper into Scripture to gain a greater understanding. Examining the wording more closely, we can see that they will be protected from the hurt and pain *caused* by those in the second death. In other words, hell-bound people can create a disruption for believers.

Yet those who overcome—who keep the faith when their faithfulness is tested by trials and tribulations—will be protected by hell's schemes. The sinners bound for hell will not be allowed to mess them up any longer. They will not be allowed to destroy their fellowship with God. They will not be allowed to take them down. To put it in contemporary context, hell-bound people won't be able to "cancel" Christians and cause them to lose their reward.

The cancel culture has taken the cost of living the public Christian life to a whole new level. Saying the wrong thing just once, people have lost entire careers. Plus, what the "wrong" thing is can change on a dime. But the encouragement given to those tested in Smyrna is that if they hold fast to their faith to the end, they will be saved when cancel culture pulls their membership card. They don't need to be afraid of the threats of others, because part of their reward is living in the safety and protection of the King of kings, who has placed the crown of life on them.

As you consider your stand for Jesus Christ—whether on the job, in your relationships, on social media, or wherever—know that you may face difficulties as a result of your public proclamation of Him. You may face dark days. You may face isolation or even monetary loss. But if you hold on to your faith in Jesus Christ and remain steadfast, immovable, and always faithful to Him, He will guard you and protect you from a hell-bound society that seems hell-bent on destroying people who name the name of Christ. His covering is your protection, and His covering is accessed through your faithful commitment to Him. Your commitment must be to Christ.

But if you fail, just stop and confess—repent—and then step onto the road to faithfulness. Don't throw in the towel. Don't quit. You're not only here to be a disciple but to help others become disciples too. You're here to say, like Paul did, "I am not ashamed of the gospel, for it is the power of God for salvation to everyone who believes, to the Jew first and also to the Greek" (Romans 1:16). You are to profess the name of Jesus regularly, wisely, and clearly.

And when trouble comes as a result, keep your eyes on Him. Hang on. Buckle up. Be faithful. He will be with you in the pain and waiting for you at the end with a crown of life and all the rights and privileges that go with that position.

4

EMBRACING UNCOMPROMISING COMMITMENT

THE CHURCH IN PERGAMUM
(Revelation 2:12-17)

Have you ever driven behind someone who wasn't quite sure which highway lane they wanted to use? Sometimes they stayed in your lane, but then they'd shift to another one. Sometimes, at least for a few seconds, they'd straddle two lanes. To say this person was indecisive would be an understatement.

You need to know two things in a situation like that. The first—obviously—is that the driver is confused. The second is that everyone behind them is now confused. Whenever someone is unstable about which "lane" to take in life, they inevitably create instability for others as well.

But what does this have to do with the church in Pergamum? Well, they had a commitment problem too. But first let's look at the environment in which they lived.

Through the angel commissioned to communicate His message, Jesus told the church, "I know where you dwell, where Satan's throne is" (Revelation 2:13). Pergamum was the capital of the satanic. And as you may recall, the church in Smyrna had similar surroundings, said to be dwelling in the synagogue of Satan (Revelation 2:9). But here Jesus takes it a step further. He states that Pergamum is smack-dab in the center of Satan's throne room itself. They're in a dire predicament.

Then Jesus follows with a message about overcoming—about how to live above the culture, chaos, and quagmire around them: "You hold fast My name, and did not deny My faith even in the days of Antipas, My witness, My faithful one, who was killed among you, where Satan dwells" (verse 13). Jesus is saying the key to experiencing eternal victory in the midst of an earthly experience that's not so ideal comes in one word: commitment. And not just commitment, but uncompromising commitment. He's saying if the people of the church in Pergamum want to overcome, they must be uncompromising Christians. Because compromise and commitment cannot coincide.

This is similar to the confused driver I mentioned earlier. Drivers can't commit to a certain lane while simultaneously compromising on which lane to use. It has to be one or the other. The two are mutually exclusive. And Jesus says uncompromising commitment must be the goal, especially for those surrounded by an enormous amount of compromise.

Let's step back to how Jesus introduces Himself to this church.

JESUS' DESIGNATION—THE TWO-EDGED SWORD

Jesus presents this key to the church in Pergamum by first introducing Himself with a certain designation. As we study the seven churches in Revelation, it's important to keep in mind that each one receives a different designation of Christ's character and qualities, the very first part of each message. Here, Jesus introduces Himself with "the One who has the sharp two-edged sword" (2:12). This designation refers back to Revelation 1:16: "In His right hand He held seven stars, and out of His mouth came a sharp two-edged sword; and His face was like the sun shining in its strength."

Why does Jesus introduce Himself this way? Because Pergamum is steep in the worship of the Roman State. Rome is the dominant influence of Asia Minor, where all seven of these churches are located, and that means they're ruled by the Roman sword. And a sword in biblical times indicated authority.

For example, Romans 13:4 references the government as "bearing the sword," which means to act as a legal representative. Thus, with Satan controlling the capital, politicians, and powers in Pergamum, it was quite normative for the Christians' reaction at being forced to bow to Caesar and adopt secular religious practices to be consternation and concern. And we know this is so because Jesus refers to a believer named Antipas who refused to bow to the powers that be, and it cost him his life. He was a martyr for the faith. So quite naturally in this arena of uncertainty, there would be a spirit of fear.

What we should remember, though, is that when fear creeps up, we need to look to God and His sovereign hand. We should never allow the emotion of fear to turn into a spirit of fear by letting it linger.

To the Pergamum believers who had fears, then, Jesus Christ comes on the scene and offers His own designation to address their fears. He is the One who has the sharp two-edged sword, and the reason He offers this first and foremost is that He asks them to do something as a result. He asks them to choose which authority to fear most.

Do you fear the power of the man and his sword? Or do you fear the power of Jesus and His—His Word? What Jesus is purporting in this opening statement is that His authority is greater than the authorities that cause us to fear the most. Even if we're terrified or threatened, or the circumstances and people around us are causing our life to be difficult, Jesus reminds us that the key to overcoming is acknowledging and abiding in the truth that He has authority over all. In Matthew 28:18 He said, "All authority has been given to Me in heaven and on earth."

Man may have *a* word, but mankind never has the *final* word—even in the most challenging of times. No ruler, boss, company, owner, supervisor, spouse, neighbor, friend, doctor, enemy, family member—no one—overrules God. All people act by God's permission and never by their own command because God sits as King over all. He is the potentate of the universe. What's more, He has a sword and the divinely ordained authority to use it.

Hebrews 4:12 says, "The word of God is living and active and sharper than any two-edged sword, and piercing as far as the division of soul and spirit, of both joints and marrow, and able to judge the thoughts and intentions of the heart." God's Word pierces and penetrates in its ability and power to effect change for good or for judgment.

The problem today is that far too many Christians have lost faith in the power of the sword, which comes from Jesus' mouth. I'm not saying that the Bible is disrespected. It's not. We often carry it around or place it in a prominent place in our home. But I am saying it's often dismissed. The authority of the words within it are marginalized in our lives and decisions.

What Jesus wanted the Christians in Pergamum to know is that His Word is the final word on all things. It's the authoritative sword. He wanted to remind them of this truth before addressing the issue at hand:

> I have a few things against you, because you have there some who hold the teaching of Balaam, who kept teaching Balak to put a stumbling block before the sons of Israel, to eat things sacrificed to idols and to commit acts of immorality. So you also have some who in the same way hold the teaching of the Nicolaitans (Revelation 2:14-15).

Jesus stated the problem clearly. While the church claimed Jesus, they compromised, and while they said they were Christian, they tolerated the compromise of the Nicolaitans, a clearly heretical Christian sect. They tolerated the compromise of others. The issue with this church was a lack of conviction. Conviction leads to commitment, but the lack of commitment leads to compromise.

Let's look at what we should know about the lack of commitment, misunderstanding and misusing grace, and the cost of compromise.

THE LACK OF COMMITMENT

In Numbers chapters 22–25, we see that Israel was moving forward in their settling of the land God had given them, and Balak, the king of Moab, was frightened by how large and powerful this group had grown. He had to do something to slow them down, so he contacted a prophet named Balaam and paid him to speak a curse over them as if it were from God Himself.

Balaam didn't mind profiting as a prophet, so he took the money, hopped onto his donkey, and started on his way. That's when the angel of the Lord stood in front of his donkey. Animals are sensitive creatures, and this one began to back up. Balaam didn't see the angel, so he thought the donkey was just being stubborn and struck it in an effort to get him to move forward.

This took place a few times along the path, one time pinning Balaam's leg against a wall when the donkey moved closer to it to avoid the angel. Eventually, the donkey grew tired of being hit, and according to Numbers 22:28, he turned to Balaam and said, "What have I done to you, that you have struck me these three times?"

I'm not sure which startles me more—that a donkey talked to a prophet or that the prophet replied. But in verse 29 we read Balaam's response: "Because you have made a mockery of me! If there had been a sword in my hand, I would have killed you by now."

Obviously, the two of them were in it pretty deep by then, as the conversation only escalated in verse 30: "The donkey said to Balaam, 'Am I not your donkey on which you have ridden all your life to this day? Have I ever been accustomed to do so to you?' And he said, 'No.'"

I would have loved to see God's expression as He witnessed this whole exchange between Balaam and his donkey. But we know He had enough because of what we read in verse 31: "Then the LORD opened the eyes of Balaam, and he saw the angel of the LORD standing in the way with his drawn sword in his hand; and he bowed all the way to the ground." God let Balaam know he was not to curse the Israelites, because they were God's people. He had to go back to Balak and tell him he couldn't do it.

Balak knew God's character couldn't stand compromise, and He also knew Israelites would face God's consequences if they did compromise. So then he tried to get the people to behave in such a way that they would bring God's wrath upon themselves, essentially inviting their own curse through their actions. In Revelation 2:14, Jesus reminds the church at Pergamum that Balak, through the teachings of Ballam, "put a stumbling block before the sons of Israel," drawing them into sin, including idolatry. They fell for it hook, line, and sinker.

Now, years later, the church in Pergamum was experiencing the same compromise. They were holding to the teachings of the Nicolaitans, who used grace as a license to sin and compromise with idolatry and immorality (Acts 15:28-29). What's more, those who were not compromising themselves were tolerating compromise in others, and as a result, the church was infected with compromise. It was a compromise of standards, morals, and even deities.

To put it another way, they misunderstood grace.

MISUNDERSTANDING AND MISUSING GRACE

One of the greatest words in the Christian language is *grace*. Grace refers to God's unmerited favor. It is all that God has done for us independent of us. But what grace does not refer to is a license to sin. We are not free to sin because of grace; that's a misuse of grace. As Paul states in Romans 6:1, "What shall we say then? Are we to continue in sin so that grace may increase?" Stated differently it could read, "Do we increase our sin because we know God forgives?" In that sense, grace becomes an excuse to sin. Yet that is both a misunderstanding of what grace is and a misuse of the word.

Grace doesn't free a person *to* sin; grace frees a person *from* sin. And grace teaches us to deny ungodliness as explained in Titus 2:

> The grace of God has appeared, bringing salvation to all men, instructing us to deny ungodliness and worldly desires and to live sensibly, righteously and godly in the present age, looking for the blessed hope and the appearing of the glory of our great God and Savior, Christ Jesus, who gave Himself for us to redeem us from every lawless deed, and to purify for Himself a people for His own possession, zealous for good deeds (verses 11-14).

The grace of God is given to free you from compromise, not to make you feel comfortable with compromise. When someone uses grace as an excuse to sin, it is either not understood or not applied. The church in Pergamum was letting the Nicolaitans off the hook by helping them feel comfortable in their compromise. But that's a dangerous stand, because it can lead to dangerous results. If a driver was swerving all over the road, would you let them feel comfortable in their compromise? No. You would honk or even call the cops because their compromise in not obeying the rules of the road was putting not only themselves but everyone else in danger.

THE COST OF COMPROMISE

Sin puts the person committing the sin and others in their path in danger of the consequences sin produces. There's a false view in Christian circles that we are not to judge sin or call sin out. But that isn't accurate. We are not to judge *people*, and we are not to judge *preferences* (Romans 14:1-12), but principles not based on God's Word are to be judged based on His Word. You are to love the sinner but hate the sin. Love is not enabling someone to continue in their own self-destruction. It's compassionately and righteously pursuing the well-being of another.

A lot of people attend church to hook up with like-minded people and feel spiritually comfortable. But one job of the church is to provide an atmosphere of spiritual comfort, another is to provide a loving place for spiritual correction. You need both in order to grow in God's grace and live according to His principles. The church is to bring God's Word to its members, even when their lifestyles disagree with His Word.

As we discussed earlier, the Word of God is like a sword, and last I checked, a sword cuts. The Word of God should be given the opportunity to cut through the lies and deception of this world in order to produce righteous living and kingdom values in Christ's followers.

A refusal to compromise can cost you money if you live in a culture that embraces it as the norm. It can cost you relationships. It can cost you societal good standing, giving you notoriety instead. In fact, it can cost you your life, as we saw it cost a man named Antipas his life. But God calls us to live a life without compromise. He calls us to a life of commitment based on conviction, founded on the truths given to us in His Word.

You can't be like the hunter who came across a bear and the beast held up a paw and said, "Wait a minute. Why do you want to shoot me?"

"Because I'm cold, and I want a fur coat."

"Well, look. Before you shoot me, can we negotiate? Let's have a meal together first. You're cold. I'm hungry. So let's just pause and talk about this."

You can imagine how that meeting turned out after the hunter agreed to this proposal. And I can assure you the bear was no longer hungry. Similarly, Satan will often look to negotiate with you when it comes to living your life for Jesus Christ. He looks for ways to get you to compromise. That's because he wants to eat you for dinner, and compromise is the surest way to turn yourself into the devil's next meal.

God doesn't want a little bit of His Word and a little bit of the world stirred together into something palatable to your lifestyle. That's like putting a spoonful of poison into a pot of soup. You wouldn't compromise with poison in your soup, eating it anyway. Neither does God want you to compromise with Satan's worldview and values in your life choices.

We're living in a day when more and more churches are compromising to please the world. They're compromising with same-sex marriage. They're compromising with embracing the transgender movement. They're compromising on the sanctity of life with abortion. They're compromising on a myriad of clear biblical standards God has set up as though they're open for negotiation.

But the Word of God is not open for negotiation. There is to be no negotiation when God has spoken clearly on a subject. In fact, every question has only two answers: God's answer through His Word and everybody else's. And when everybody else disagrees with God, everybody else is wrong. God has spoken, and He has not stuttered.

The church in Pergamum was called out because of their compromise. Despite their efforts to serve God. Despite their obedience in other areas. Despite their own personal sacrifices and commitment. It's like poison in that pot of soup. You don't eat the soup if a spoonful of poison has been tossed in. Jesus wanted them know they needed to get rid of the poison. They needed to remove the compromise.

THE NEED TO REPENT

In Revelation 2:16, Jesus then told the Pergamum church, "Repent; or else I am coming to you quickly, and I will make war against them with the sword of My mouth." The church was being warned that war would come against the Nicolaitans if they didn't stop teaching false doctrines. They were being called upon to give up their compromising stance with them and hold them accountable. If they cared about the Nicolaitans at all, they would want to spare them from the judgment about to befall them.

This is an interesting scenario. The war would be against the Nicolaitans, not the church members. Instead they were being warned that if they didn't repent of their compromise and call their so-called friends to account, that's when the war would be unleashed. And when war comes, everyone is impacted. Jesus told them to deal with it, or He would. They needed to repent of tolerating unhealthy and toxic behavior. They needed to repent of accepting the compromises of others. They needed to repent of living as enablers.

Then in verse 17, Jesus' message follows up with, "He who has an ear, let him hear what the Spirit says to the churches. To him who overcomes, to him I will give some of the hidden manna, and I will give him a white stone, and a new name written on the stone which no one knows but he who receives it."

MISSING THE MANNA

The people who overcame the temptation to compromise or tolerate compromise and instead operated by divine conviction were to receive hidden manna. Manna was a food sent by God, previously unknown, to the Israelites during their years in the wilderness. It gave substance to all those who ate it. The word translated means "What is it?" No one knew, but this supernatural provision of God allowed the Israelites to survive what would have otherwise been death by starvation in the wilderness. Once they had settled in the fertile land, they were to remember this provision of manna. Some of it was saved in the ark of the covenant to serve as a reminder of God's provision when they had nothing to eat at all.

The hidden manna promised to those who overcome the temptation to compromise refers to God's unseen provision. The Israelites in the wilderness didn't know where the manna came from. To them, it came from heaven. The source was hidden. Similarly, when God intervenes to provide during dire times in your life, it often comes from a location you would never suspect. And God's hidden provisions usually show up just when we need them the most.

The problem is this: If you're living a life of compromise, God will not release His provision into your life like He would if you were a faithful kingdom follower. Compromise always costs you something. You may not know what it costs you, but it always limits God's supply of hidden manna into your life and circumstances. Hidden manna is for those who are committed in their walk with God and won't condone the ongoing sinfulness of those around them. They will call out the sin for what it is, and as a result, they receive God's supply.

If you've ever flown on a plane, you know flight attendants sometimes pull a curtain behind the front first class section, hiding it from the rest of the passengers in coach. Then if they serve a meal, it's not for everyone on the plane. It's a special meal for special passengers who are now hidden from all the other passengers. Similarly, God has hidden manna He will supply to those who serve Him faithfully and overcome the temptation to compromise or tolerate compromise.

But He won't force you to sit where you can receive it. You choose to sit in the special area by your choices and your obedience to Him. It's not enough to just say you believe in Jesus or to show up where He is or to attend church. Jesus knows your heart. He knows if you are committed or if you compromise—and if you tolerate other people's compromise.

John 2:23-25 shows us how God views our hearts:

> When [Jesus] was in Jerusalem at the Passover, during the
> feast, many believed in His name, observing His signs which
> He was doing. But Jesus, on His part, was not entrusting
> Himself to them, for He knew all men, and because He
> did not need anyone to testify concerning man, for He
> Himself knew what was in man.

What God has in the Christian culture today are a lot of uncom-
mitted saved people. Lots of Christians claim to love God on Sunday
but then compromise by Sunday afternoon. They love God when they
praise Him during church, but they love the world in their weekly
activities. These are the believers who, if they were accused of being
a Christian, would not provide enough evidence to convict them.
They compromise their faith either through actions and words out
of alignment with God's Word or by tolerating others who compromise—or both. As a result, they relinquish any right or opportunity
to gain the hidden manna from above, God's provision when they
need it most.

MISSING YOUR SPECIAL ACCESS

Not only does the reward of provision when you need it most
become limited or eliminated in the midst of compromise, but God
says you will miss out on something else as well. You will miss out
on receiving the white stone with a name nobody else knows. It's a
secret name between you and God. It opens doors for you. It allows
you to enter places others cannot. Like a VIP badge at a special event,
your name written on a white stone is your access to a deeper, more
intimate relationship with God Himself. Overcoming the sin of compromise or the tolerance of other people's compromise brings you

both temporal and eternal rewards. You receive the hidden provision of God when you need it most, and you gain access into His inner sanctuary by virtue of a secret name He's given to you.

The church in Pergamum had a lot going for them, but their sin of compromise and tolerating the compromise of others limited their experience of God's divine provision and favor. We can learn from their example and take seriously the call to a higher level of commitment to obeying God's rule in our lives, as well as to sharing the truth of God's Word with those around us so they don't continue in compromise either.

When you get to heaven, millions of believers will kneel around God's throne, and you want to be one whose name is called. You want to be one whose name is written on the white stone. But for this to happen, you need to hold fast to your commitment to follow Christ wholeheartedly and speak up for His rule both in and over all.

5

VIEWING SIN GOD'S WAY

THE CHURCH IN THYATIRA
(Revelation 2:18-29)

The opportunity for advancement is one of the reasons living in America is so enticing to people around the world, even with all of its flaws and weaknesses. The structure of our nation offers everyone the chance to take an idea and then, within appropriate boundaries, maximize it for growth.

This comes with being part of a capitalistically based democracy, where you can use your own ingenuity, striving to achieve your best in business. And this is why we live in a continually competitive environment. If someone comes up with a concept similar to yours, only better, and positions it more strategically, you must improve what you're offering or you'll go under. This environment, then, prompts both businesses and individuals to adopt a mindset of improvement.

Zero tolerance—when there is little to no room for error—is one of the standards many corporations have adopted because of this mindset. Years ago there was a concern that foreign-made vehicles could outsell American-made vehicles because so many of those companies emphasized zero tolerance in design, manufacturing, production, and performance, and this could shift consumer purchases. So American car manufacturers began raising their standards to be more competitive. Otherwise, they might not get the return they wanted. If what they offered was substandard, people could simply shop elsewhere.

Isn't it equally true that our standards should maximize our potential as Christians? Shouldn't we understand that a perfect God is less than satisfied when we offer Him less than our best as believers? Shouldn't God's standards be ours as well?

Zero tolerance means just that—zero tolerance. We accept this reality in many areas of our lives. Suppose someone took an arithmetic test that asked what one plus one is and answered "three." The teacher would mark that answer wrong. What if the student then said, "But at least I was close"? It wouldn't matter, because the teacher would have zero tolerance for mistakes on tests.

Or what if a basketball player took a shot and the heel of his shoe was on the boundary line. Even though his successful shot would have won the game, what would the referee rule—even though it was just a small portion of the player's shoe crossing the line? The referee would have zero tolerance concerning that error.

Let me bring this closer to home for those of you who don't like math or basketball but are okay with flying. What if the pilot came on the overhead announcement system and said, "Well folks, it looks like one fuel line is leaking but not all of them. So we should be good to go." You and the rest of the passengers would make a beeline for the exit before that pilot even had a chance to taxi to a runway. I imagine you would have a zero tolerance mentality when it comes to leaking fuel lines on airplanes.

When you really think about it, we function in a zero tolerance mindset more often than we realize. And if this is true for business, tests, basketball, and flying, why do we question zero tolerance when it comes to God? Is He to expect less from you and me—and from

His church? No. Yet we far too often question God's view of sin, His stand against sin.

OUR MINDSET TOWARD SIN

When Jesus sends His next message to the church in Thyatira, He wants them to know that in order for them to live as overcomers both on earth and for eternity, they need to have a zero tolerance mindset toward sin. They will need to never settle for their own sins or the sins of others. Statements like "Boys will be boys" or "I'm only human" won't be accepted as an excuse. And while there is a modicum of truth within those statements, they reflect a tolerant spirit that the Lord does not want us to have.

Far too many of us live as victims today rather than as victors. And one of the main reasons is that we tolerate too much that doesn't reflect the values of the kingdom of God either in ourselves or in others.

I'm certain you have some nonadjustable expectations. You may call them boundaries, perhaps involving how you want others to treat you. No one questions the purpose and wisdom of personal boundaries, whether in our work-life balance, our relationships, or even what we choose to view as entertainment. These boundaries exist in order to provide the most optimum environment for us to thrive.

We need to keep boundaries in mind as we explore this next church, because God also has boundaries, and He will not tolerate anyone deliberately crossing them.

WHAT THE CHURCH IN THYATIRA FACED

In Revelation 2:18—"The Son of God, who has eyes like a flame of fire, and His feet are like burnished bronze"—Jesus once again introduces Himself according to His power and strength. His eyes are like flames of fire, and His feet are powerful, similar to burnished bronze.

With this image we know we're hearing from Someone who sees all and can penetrate that sight to the depths of any being. Someone who is sturdy, foundationally secure, and unwavering.

Let's look at what Thyatira was like.

This city was located 35 miles southwest of Pergamum. It was known for the protection, promotion, and benefits offered to people who shared a similar occupation or enterprise through what were called guilds. They were similar to a steelworker's union or a teacher's union today.

And in the midst of these thriving guilds, a church had been planted as described for us in the book of Acts. It had an interesting beginning in that Paul preached to the people of the city, and a woman was one of the first to respond: "Lydia, from the city of Thyatira, a seller of purple fabrics, a worshiper of God, was listening; and the Lord opened her heart to respond to the things spoken by Paul" (Acts 16:14). From this we can discern that Lydia may have been a successful businesswoman. Purple clothing was part of the couture offering for uptown shoppers, and Lydia was a distributor of these stylish clothes. She was an industrious woman, and she found Paul's teachings intriguing.

Out of Lydia's conversion and enthusiasm for the Word of God grew a bustling church in an even more bustling city. Thyatira was a working society, but it was also a partying society. Many of the guilds carried the tone and character of a sorority or fraternity. They existed for workers' rights and recognition but also for community. Coworkers quickly became the people to party with.

The problems showed up when the Christians at this new church in Thyatira were expected to continue partying with their coworkers. It wasn't that partying was wrong in and of itself, but what took place at these parties often went against their values in the Christian faith. This created a crisis of faith for many of the Christians in that city. They were faced with a dilemma. Should they go along to get along? Or stand up for their beliefs, risking being left out or even ostracized?

Yet despite these many pressures, Jesus commends their behavior on a lot of levels: "I know your deeds, and your love and faith and service and perseverance, and that your deeds of late are greater than at first" (verse 19).

Their love, faith, service, and perseverance are all applauded. They were obviously a congregation that wanted to do the right thing, and they were seeking to grow and develop and even reach others with the good news of Jesus Christ. But even with all they had going for them, they had somehow dropped the ball.

JEZEBEL

In the next few verses, Jesus tells the church:

> But I have this against you, that you tolerate the woman Jezebel, who calls herself a prophetess, and she teaches and leads My bond-servants astray so that they commit acts of immorality and eat things sacrificed to idols. I gave her time to repent, and she does not want to repent of her immorality. Behold, I will throw her on a bed of sickness, and those who commit adultery with her into great tribulation, unless they repent of her deeds. And I will kill her children with pestilence, and all the churches will know that I am He who searches the minds and hearts; and I will give to each one of you according to your deeds (verses 20-23).

The original Jezebel was already dead, as told in 2 Kings 9:33-37. But as you can see, any "Jezebel" is not someone to tolerate. She is not someone to take lightly. Her teachings are not to be accepted in any manner. And even though the members of the church in Thyatira were doing many good things, their tolerating their Jezebel negated it all. They may not have been participating in the practices she was promoting, but simply accepting her teaching of those practices and not calling her out was enough to break God's standard.

This Jezebel went around telling people, as if from God, to live in ways that were contrary to God's revealed will. She told them it was actually all right to do these things. And because she publicly attached her teaching to that of the authority of God, she made what she said sound spiritual. She wrapped it in Christianese. She came across as holy. (She probably would have had a few bestselling books and a large social media following.)

But rather than call her out on the untruths she was spreading in God's name, the church in Thyatira simply looked the other way. They hid behind the *Your business is your business* mentality and claimed the *Who am I to judge?* clause. And as they did, her false teaching went further into the culture, drawing more and more people away from God and His truth. She was like cult leaders David Koresh in the nineties and Jim Jones in the seventies, using the name of God to lead people into sin.

The Thyatira church's failure to publicly condemn this false teaching and point out what was untrue was what got them called out and confronted. They were told it was their business to stand up to false teachers and false teaching done in God's name. They were reminded that secretly living as a Christian is not how the Christian life is to be lived. You must be clear on where you stand if you are to be a follower of Jesus Christ. You must have a right mindset toward sin that's a reflection of God's zero tolerance.

The history of the name Jezebel and all it means goes back to 1 Kings, chapters 16 and 17. Jezebel was married to Ahab, the king of Israel, making her queen. She was also the daughter of a king. What's more, she was a known worshiper of Baal, the fertility god and the god of pagans, and she had lured her husband into worshiping Baal as well. She was a cunning, strong-willed individual who manipulated her husband to compromise. And as he compromised, all of Israel was led into a lifestyle of compromise too.

Jezebel had such a powerful influence that she even threatened the prophet of God, Elijah. She told him she had 850 prophets and that if he kept doing what he was doing, she would have him killed. Basically, she let Elijah know she was ruling the roost. Her husband had the title, and she had the power.

This church's tolerating a Jezebel in their midst was allowing a shameful powerbroker to mislead the people who were just coming to Christ. They were allowing the dumbing down of God's standard and the twisting of His truth. To this day, mentioning a Jezebel teaching is a reference to this double-minded mixture of religion and rule. But Christians are not to be tolerant of sin when it comes to God's Word and His standards set there.

Far too many churches and believers today, however, have become tolerant in our contemporary culture, which is similar to the one in Thyatira, hoping to be popular, fill pews, or make people comfortable with their sinful views. Tolerance has turned into a cardinal virtue as an effort to increase church membership, bring in financial support, or grow an online presence with an extended base of followers. Yet God says tolerance of any kind of sin is unacceptable. What is unacceptable to God by way of behaviors or sin ought to be unacceptable to everyone who calls themselves His followers.

OUR CHALLENGE TODAY

We live in a day when people are constantly dumbing down God's standards. That's not to say that any of us are perfect or live perfectly. But to tolerate sin is to enable it, whether in our own lives or in others'.

When you're sick, you don't simply tolerate your symptoms; you look for a solution. A cure. If your sickness becomes severe or even life-threatening, you head to the ER. Had I just resigned myself to tolerate the pneumonia I developed during the COVID-19 pandemic, I probably wouldn't be writing this book right now. Tolerating what has gone wrong in our bodies only leads to greater issues down the road. Similarly, tolerating what has gone wrong spiritually in our lives—and in our culture—only leads to greater spiritual collapse and chaos.

What if you were wheeled into an operating room with instruments that looked dirty? Would you feel comfortable going ahead with your surgery? Would you be willing to tolerate those germs? No one should have to tolerate that, because once you're cut open, exposure to even a few germs can eventually prove deadly. That's why medical facilities have elaborate systems to sterilize not only their equipment but their operating rooms as well. Germs are not to be tolerated. That doesn't make the doctors and nurses mean and *intolerant*—generally a pejorative, judgmental term. It makes them wise and able to help you heal so you can experience your best life.

The church of Jesus Christ is supposed to act as a hospital where spiritually sick people can find healing for their soul and emotional wounds. We are not supposed to be a hospice where we simply make people comfortable while they die. Yet it has become more of the norm for churches to just want people to feel comfortable as they continue in unhealthy behavior and sin. They want them to feel good for a moment rather than healed for good.

But tolerating the distortion of God's truth in any form leads to destruction in the church, and a Jezebel teaching of idolatry comes with consequences. Those who follow her lead today will reap the consequences of their own choices. Satan knows this. It's why he's strategically placed those like Jezebel in so many churches—so they'll subtly lead people astray. Jezebel didn't just show up in Thyatira; she's very present even now in churches all across our land as well as across the world.

Keep in mind, this Jezebel's misleading teachings did not come from a heart of naivete. As we saw in Revelation 2:21, God had given her a chance: "I gave her time to repent, and she does not want to repent of her immorality." Sin is bad. But not wanting to repent is even worse, because now the person has entered into a space of rebellion. Rebellion is a whole different scenario than sinning in and of itself. Rebellion is a commitment to the sin. Jezebel wasn't struggling to overcome something that had gained a foothold in her life; she was a rebel. She was influencing others to live as rebels too. And she wasn't being called out for it.

But how do we live out this right mindset toward sin that reflects God's own?

Biblically Call Out Open Sin

As I mentioned before, we are not to judge the sinner, just the sin. But people often confuse the two and don't do either. Calling out open sin in a person's life is a legitimate thing to do, though biblically, lovingly, and responsibly. Each person's actions must stand up to the scrutiny of God's standards, because if they don't and they remain in the sin, God will carry out His wrath in their life. Pointing out the sin is a loving thing to do when it's done in a way that can help the person break free from it.

Romans 11:22 reminds us that God is not just a God of rainbows and cupcakes. He's a God who is kind but also severe. In this verse Paul says, "Behold then the kindness and severity of God; to those who fell, severity, but to you, God's kindness, if you continue in His kindness; otherwise you also will be cut off."

God has two sides—one of love and blessing and one of wrath and severity. Unfortunately, most people just want the love side of God. They just want the blessing side of God. But God is also a God of wrath and severity. And again, one of the most loving things you can do for someone is to point out their sin to help them avoid the consequences of that sin. Truth and love must be kept together as you serve God as His kingdom disciple. You cannot give up truth for love. Nor can you give up love for truth. You have to hold them simultaneously, because that reflects God's standard.

Address Personal Rebellion or Suffer the Consequences

Tolerating the rebellion of others, especially when that rebellion is being taught as truth under God's name, is to dismiss God's standard. It's to become a participant in the ushering in of sin's consequences. But as we saw in Jesus' message, personal rebellion brings personal consequences. The consequences this Jezebel was bringing on herself would be severe—she would be thrown onto a bed of sickness and put into a time of great tribulation.

Here's a graphic description of the original Jezebel's death from 2 Kings 9:33-37:

> [The prophet Jehu] said, "Throw her down." So they threw her down, and some of her blood was sprinkled on the wall and on the horses, and he trampled her under foot. When he came in, he ate and drank; and he said, "See now to this cursed woman and bury her, for she is a king's daughter." They went to bury her, but they found nothing more of her than the skull and the feet and the palms of her hands. Therefore they returned and told him. And he said, "This is the word of the LORD, which He spoke by His servant Elijah the Tishbite, saying, 'In the property of Jezreel the dogs shall eat the flesh of Jezebel; and the corpse of Jezebel will be as dung on the face of the field in the property of Jezreel, so they cannot say, "This is Jezebel."'"

"Oh how the mighty have fallen" takes on a whole new meaning when it comes to Jezebel. God did not tolerate her open rebellion nor her using that rebellion to lead others astray. To be eaten by dogs was a disgrace. And yet that is what God allowed for the woman who openly disobeyed Him and taught others to disobey and dishonor His rules. And He would allow similar consequences for the Jezebel in Thyatira. Furthermore, the consequences wouldn't stop with her. Jesus said her children would also suffer as a result of her rebellion.

Take a Stand

At one time in our American culture, biblical values were at least supported or tolerated. But today many biblical values are dishonored. Not only are they rejected, but their rejection is flaunted all over our entertainment and in our culture itself. The opposition to Christ and His kingdom values has become a very public dismissal in a whole number of areas. In many ways, then, we are similar to the church in Thyatira. We have believers who are persevering and show love and faithfulness, but very few stand up to the open and outright spiritual rebellion taking place throughout our land, society, schools, churches, communities, and entertainment industries.

There must be a standard that those of us in the kingdom of God hold to and uphold. If we drift out of alignment under Christ, the culture will have no bearing at all. We are the standard bearers for marriage, culture, relationships, integrity, grace, and more. Without this, we are no better than the church in Thyatira. We are tolerating the Jezebels in our midst, and the message to those who tolerate false teaching is a harsh one. Just as Jezebel and her children suffered from her rebellious ways, so will those who tolerate sin and rebellion among them.

OUR REWARD

Yet God had another message for the church in Thyatira, this time for those who did not give in to the temptation to tolerate rebellion, immoral behavior, and false teaching in His name. We read it in verses 24-25: "I say to you, the rest who are in Thyatira, who do not hold this teaching, who have not known the deep things of Satan, as they call them—I place no other burden on you. Nevertheless what you have, hold fast until I come."

This raises a question: What are the deep things of Satan? For starters, any invitation to disobey God. We all face that. And we have all given in to that invitation at some point or another. Whenever we've disobeyed God in our thoughts, words, and actions, we've obeyed Satan. But a "deep" thing of Satan goes beyond that. It's when you rebel. It's when you begin to call evil good (Isaiah 5:20). You don't just sin; rather, you dive to the bottom of Satan's pit and hang out with him. You make his home your own and seek to influence others to do the same. When this takes place, you are living like a Jezebel.

But for those who don't accept the teaching of the deep things of Satan—for those who do not call what is evil as good—the message is clear. There is no greater burden on them. No greater burden is placed. In essence, God's commands will no longer be burdensome to them. And if this is you, you will be free to live the Christian life with the ease of His presence. As we read in 1 John 5:3, "For this is the love of God, that we keep His commandments; and His commandments are not burdensome." Because of God's love present in you as you stand up for His truth, His commandments will not be a burden to you. When God is on your side, He will come through for you in ways you never even imagined possible.

That's why the church members at Thyatira are told to "hold fast" until Christ comes. They are to hang in there and know that even if they face difficulties at work, in the community, or with relationships because they're not tolerating the guilds' ways or the societal leaders' values or their Jezebel's teaching, God will show up for them when they need Him most. And not only will He show up for them, but He will bring them a reward.

The message to this church planted in the midst of a difficult culture concludes with the following promises:

> He who overcomes, and he who keeps My deeds until the end, to him I will give authority over the nations; and he shall rule them with a rod of iron, as the vessels of the potter are broken to pieces, as I also have received authority from My Father; and I will give him the morning star (verses 26-28).

The church is told to expect some help in the here and now, but this as well: If they hold out and stay true by standing up for God's standard in society and against false teachers of the faith, they will also get a reward in both this life and the life to come.

They will be given the ability to rule with God, along with the gift of the morning star. That means when they choose to take their stand with love and kindness but also with clarity, God will lift them up in their spiritual authority. He will strengthen them in their spiritual walk. He will guide them with the light of the morning star. This is a unique intimate experience with Christ through His Word (2 Peter 1:19). They will gain insights on how to move forward in a culture that rewards playing the games their guilds put forth. He will open doors for them, while at the same time strengthen them spiritually to overcome all they face.

That reward is also ours whenever we make the divine standard of God the standard we hold to and proclaim at all costs. When we have conviction and the right mindset toward sin God expects.

6

WALKING IN THE SPIRIT'S POWER

THE CHURCH IN SARDIS
(Revelation 3:1-6)

A man was visiting his neighbor's pig farm one day when he noticed something unusual about one of the pigs. It seemed to have a limp. So he moved closer to get a better view and realized the pig had a prosthetic leg. Now, he'd never seen anything like that before—a pig with an artificial limb! So he asked the farmer why this pig was so special.

The farmer just smiled and explained that one day his granddaughter was walking in front of a tractor when the tractor was about to hit her. This pig jumped in and knocked her out of the way. On another occasion, his grandson was drowning, and this pig jumped into the water and saved him.

The man was awed at the heroic feats of this pig. He smiled and told the farmer that he understood why he would want to give this pig, who had no doubt been injured in one of those rescues, an artificial limb.

But the farmer just chuckled. "Oh no," he said, "the pig wasn't injured at all. I just didn't have the heart to eat him all at one time."

Things are certainly not always as they appear. They're not always as clearly definable as they initially look. And that's why the message to the church in Sardis is as it is. The church suffered from a false sense of security. They had rested their hopes on what they could see, but what they saw was not all there was to be seen, as we will discover.

THE CITY OF SARDIS

Located just 30 miles south of Thyatira in the same general vicinity of Asia Minor, Sardis was built on a high mountain where the people had constructed an acropolis that made the city appear impregnable. It looked as if there was no way anyone could defeat this community on a hill simply because of all the trouble they would have to go through in order to do so. Yet Sardis was overthrown on two occasions: once around 547 BC by Cyrus the Great, and then again around 213 BC by Antiochus III. Both their armies came during the night—the most unsuspected time—and hit Sardis with a surprise attack.

Wouldn't nighttime be a naturally vulnerable time, and therefore, wouldn't the city especially position its guards then? You would think so. But the attacks were successful because Sardis had become so comfortable with their own sufficiency and security, believing their city was indeed impregnable. They assumed nothing could happen to them. And what was true of Sardis the city became true of Sardis the church.

THE CHURCH'S MISTAKE

This is why Jesus opens His message to the church in Sardis with this reminder of Himself: "He who has the seven Spirits of God and the seven stars" (Revelation 3:1). Remember, the number seven is the number of completion. By referring to Himself as having the seven Spirits of God, Jesus means He contains the complete work of the Holy Spirit.

This is so important to notice, because the root of the problem these Christians in Sardis had was that they had become so self-sufficient in their own minds that they didn't feel they needed the Holy Spirit anymore. They believed they could do everything on their own, which is a very dangerous position to take.

Do you know why we Christians don't pray more than we do? Because too many of us believe we're self-sufficient. We don't feel like we need God until an emergency comes up. The Christians in Sardis were educated, affluent, and at ease—very similar to those in much of our contemporary Christian culture today. As a result, they relied too heavily on themselves and became blind to the enemy's surprise attacks.

One of the greatest dangers of success—whether it's financial, status, relational, career, or anything else—is that the higher you go up the ladder, the more independent you can become. Why pray when, for example, you have an unlimited access to cash or credit? Success often lends itself to a spirit of independence that involves God only in emergencies, and as I said, this is a dangerous place to be in. It's similar to a championship-winning sports team trying to repeat their win two years in a row. Rarely does this happen, because success tends to breed complacency.

Not only were the Christians in Sardis feeling self-sufficient, but so were their pastors and spiritual leaders. We know this because Jesus also introduces Himself as the One who has the seven stars. Stars are a reference to the spiritual leaders. This reveals that there was a void of quality leadership in the church. The leadership that should have been setting the pace for the congregation to follow in terms of grabbing onto and pursuing the work of the Spirit had been setting the wrong pace of independence and ease.

A mist in the pulpit is always a fog in the pew. When spiritual leaders fail to model and teach biblical truth, their failure is magnified in the lives of those who attend their churches.

We'll soon see it's clear that the Christians in Sardis were looking to their own self-interests rather than seeking to be close to the Spirit. One of the Holy Spirit's jobs is to energize and fuel your spiritual life, but another is to make sure Satan doesn't have his way with you. It's to give you the tools you need to access the victory you want in what you're trying to overcome. But the Holy Spirit doesn't do His work apart from your connection and cooperation to Him and with Him. A life devoid of the Spirit of God is a life open to defeat in every area. It's just a matter of time.

SPIRITUAL DEATH

Here's what Jesus' message said to the church next: "I know your deeds, that you have a name that you are alive, but you are dead" (Revelation 3:1).

While Sardis was the church of what's happening now (the "in" place to worship that had the best musical lineup, hottest preaching, and fanciest buildings, not to mention the free coffee), it had missed what mattered most. They had forgotten to include the Holy Spirit as both the spiritual leader and guide for all they were to do. Sardis was a stellar church. It was well-known. It carried a positive reputation online. People streamed its services from all around.

But Revelation 3:1 lets us know they had a problem: Even though the people and community thought the church was "alive," God declared them spiritually dead. Even though their reputation and reviews said they were filled with the best spiritual small groups around, He declared otherwise. Like many churches today, it was full of comatose members.

So for all of us living today, it's possible to look like we're spiritually alive, dress like we're spiritually alive, walk like it and talk like it, and yet be comatose in the things of Christ—spiritually dead. This happens to people when they lack the fullness of the Spirit made manifest in their lives. It is the full presence of the Spirit that breathes life.

Thus, if the Holy Spirit is not operating in your life, your home, your church—even in your thoughts—there is no spiritual life in you. Study without the Spirit is a waste of time. Programming without the person of Christ made real through the Holy Spirit is a waste of time. It is the Spirit who produces both in you and through you the work of God in your life.

Let's say you buy a brand-new refrigerator with all the bells and whistles. You name it, and this refrigerator can do it. You're very excited about your new appliance, and you have it delivered and properly positioned. Then you buy plenty of fresh and frozen food to put in it. Yet when you open your refrigerator the next day, the ice cream has melted and the milk has spoiled. Instead of the smell of delicious food, there's a stench.

Now, keep in mind, you paid a lot of money for this refrigerator. Then on top of that, you paid a lot of money for the groceries that filled it. So not only do you feel like you've wasted your money on the new refrigerator but you've wasted your money on all that food now gone bad.

That's why you sound somewhat evangelically ticked-off when you pick up your phone and call the customer care team at the refrigerator manufacturer to complain about your purchase. You also ask for a replacement, but before they'll say they're willing to provide one, they want to send someone to your house to inspect the one you have. You agree, only for the representative to discover the real problem at hand.

"There's nothing wrong with your refrigerator," the inspector says. "Except for the fact that you didn't plug it in!" In other words, you don't have an equipment problem nor a manufacturer problem; you have a power problem due to your own neglect. And no matter how expensive and great your new refrigerator is, it won't work without connection to the power source it was equipped to receive.

Everyone who has accepted Jesus Christ as Savior has received the equipment they need to experience the overcoming life. Second Corinthians 5:17 tells us that everyone who is in Christ is a new creation. As a kingdom follower of Jesus, you have been given the Holy Spirit, who is there to infuse your spirit, your soul. Your soul is then equipped to infuse your body. Everything you need has been supplied. So if your Christian life isn't working, it's not due to faulty equipment; it's due to the Spirit of God not being plugged into your spirit. It's not being allowed to do the sevenfold work, the complete work, in your life and ministry. You must maintain a close and abiding connection with the Spirit in order to access His power within you.

This is one of the primary reasons many believers today find their spiritual lives lacking. Yet given how high a price was paid in order to offer each of us the gift of salvation through the finished work of Christ on the cross, there is really no excuse to live as a dead man walking. We have inside of us the living breath of the Spirit so that we can access all we need in order to overcome and overpower the enemy who seeks to drag us down.

WALKING IN THE SPIRIT—OR NOT

The job of the Holy Spirit, like a dimmer switch on a set of lights in your home, is to raise the light of Christ within you. In the Old Testament, it was God the Father who shone as the Superstar in humanity's grand drama. He showed up on every page. In the Gospels, this Superstar was Jesus Christ—God the Son. But once the beginning of the church age as revealed in Acts 2 hit, the Holy Spirit became the Superstar. The Spirit is the member of the Trinity carrying out the believer's work in the midst of the clash of the kingdoms on earth. He is responsible for transforming us into the image of Christ (2 Corinthians 3:17-18).

The Father sent the Son, and then the Son sent the Spirit. Thus, if no relationship to the Holy Spirit exists in your life, or if that relationship is somehow distant, strained, or dismissed, you won't experience much of Jesus. And if you don't experience much of Jesus, neither will you experience much of God the Father. If you want more of God in your life, you've got to have more of Jesus. And if you want more of Jesus in your life, you've got to have more of the Holy Spirit. Because without Him, you cannot access the full experience of the Godhead.

We are called to walk in the Spirit, but many people don't realize what that means. It means being filled with the Spirit. And in order to be filled with the Spirit, you must operate according to a spiritual grid. You must base your decisions on a spiritual perspective, or a kingdom worldview. Once you bring a non-spiritual perspective into your thoughts, words, or actions, you are no longer plugged into the Holy Spirit. You have unplugged your connection to Him and are walking according to your own will and your own way. If and when you aim to introduce a perspective contrary to the Spirit's, you are attempting to make your equipment work on your own power.

Yet the spiritual life was never designed to function on your human wisdom nor your human power. It is not designed to work without an outlet that connects you with the Spirit of God. First Corinthians 2:16 calls this connecting point living with "the mind of Christ." To live with the mind of Christ involves thinking like He thinks and responding like He would respond in order for the Spirit to be activated in whatever situation you're facing. Your new spiritual nature works within you only according to that which the Spirit quickens it to work.

Have you ever seen someone's front yard with a Beware of Dog sign on their fence, but you know there is no dog? They just put up the sign to scare away anyone who might be thinking of breaking into their home or even just trespassing on their property. Some Christians try to work without the power and protection of the Holy Spirit while thinking that carrying the sign that says they're a Christian is enough.

But the sign doesn't change the reality. It's the spiritual nature within that must be activated, or quickened, by God through His Spirit, or you will continue to be at least spiritually anemic. No sign can bring spiritual life. Neither can carrying a Bible or even attending church. While both of those are good and necessary for your Christian walk, if and when they're done apart from an abiding presence with the Spirit, they won't accomplish what they've been designed to produce.

You've probably seen or at least heard of films such as *Night of the Living Dead*, where zombies move around like living beings, but inside they're as dead as a doorknob. In fact, what's scary about a zombie movie is that they're aiming to hurt you even though they're dead. It's difficult to defend yourself against someone who's already dead.

But many Christians live spiritually dead lives while going around and hurting others in the family of God with toxic conversations or behavior. And when their conversations or behavior is addressed, they don't respond as someone who is convicted by the Spirit would. All this does is spread more pain, more hurt, and more destruction throughout the body of Christ as zombie Christians, disconnected from God's Spirit, infiltrate spiritual circles.

Without the Spirit of God quickening our thinking, actions, reactions, and emotions, we remain spiritually asleep and capable of harm, not helpfulness. Someone may look like they have the spiritual life going on, but that doesn't mean it's their reality. Remember my previous illustration about a baby hoping for sustenance from a pacifier? This is like that. When a parent tries to calm their crying, hungry baby with a pacifier, it works for a bit because the baby doesn't know any better. And anyone around her might think she's not hungry. But it's only a matter of time until the truth comes out. When the baby realizes the pacifier isn't about to produce milk, she spits it out and cries all the more.

Having a reputation like the one the Christians in Sardis had, made them and those around them think they were "all that," when they really weren't much of anything at all. There is no life when there is no connection to the Holy Spirit. As 2 Timothy 3:5 puts it, you have a "form of godliness" while denying its power. Basically, you're looking the part of a Christian without the power of a relationship with God.

If there is no reality of Jesus' work in your life, even if you know how to use all the right Christian words or sing all the worship songs, you're merely wearing a mask—dressing up like Jesus on Halloween. It doesn't matter what other people see, say, or think. It doesn't even matter if they're fooled. What matters is what God knows about you. He sees your heart, and He knows whether you're connected to Him intimately through an abiding relationship and fellowship with the Spirit.

WAKE UP!

When Jesus the risen, ascended Christ returns to His church, He wants to find the real thing. He wants authentic, faithful kingdom followers. He doesn't want jewelry that's fake—merely gold-plated, although it looks good for a while. He wants fully committed believers. And that's why next Jesus says, "Wake up, and strengthen the things that remain, which were about to die" (verse 2). Jesus is calling this church in Sardis—and all similar believers today—to wake up. It's time.

To "wake up" implies that you're asleep, and Jesus is declaring that many who claim His name are at least spiritually asleep. They're walking around in a spiritual stupor, believing whatever anyone tells them, failing to think for themselves. Failing to use the free will they've been given and choose to align their thoughts and actions underneath Christ. Jesus knows that in order to truly be His disciple, you'll need to be awake.

The problem with Sardis Bible Fellowship, as well as with many of the members of the contemporary church today, is that they started something spiritual but failed to finish it. They were lulled to sleep through temptations of ease, complacency, and even success. They began to follow Jesus, but then they quit when things got hard or inconvenient. They became so comfortable as casual Christians that there was no longer any aspiration or ambition to fully follow Christ.

In fact, they got used to being saved. They got used to being forgiven. They got used to being loved by God Himself. And anytime you get used to something, you can take it for granted. You stop striving after it as you once did. And in your Christian walk, you stop reading the Word, praying, witnessing, seeking God's heart and His guidance. You get sleepy.

GIVE GOD YOUR ALL

My favorite snack is Zapp's potato chips. But not just any flavor of Zapp's. The jalapeno flavor is my snack of choice. I've got bags of it in my desk drawer. I have them in my house. And in meetings with The Urban Alternative ministry, they often provide the Zapp's.

But recently, a problem came up. I noticed that my Zapp's had issues. Like many other items suffering from shrinkflation, the price of my Zapp's stayed the same or even went up, but the number of chips in the bag lessened. The company cut back on how many chips they put in to save costs. Not only that, but they also thinned the chips. So now I not only get half a bag of air but chips that don't quite pack the punch the thicker chips did. In essence, the manufacturer has decided to continue to charge full price while ripping off the delivery of their goods.

Jesus Christ paid full price on the cross for our salvation. His words on Calvary were, "It is finished." The Greek word here is *tetelestai*, which means "paid in full." Jesus didn't pay full price for your salvation only to be satisfied with your giving Him a life that's like half a bag of air. He paid full price because He wants a full commitment from you. Let's be honest. If you show up with half-hearted prayers, or half-hearted service, or even a half-hearted relationship, you're ripping God off.

But the Bible says that whatever we do—eat, drink, or anything at all—we're to do it to the glory of God. Not just a sliver of it for His glory. Not just a fourth of it for His glory. And not just half of it for His glory. *All of it.* And as we see in His message to the church in Sardis, Jesus asks them to give Him the things that remain. He asks them to give what they've been holding out.

What in your life remains? What are you keeping back for yourself? What are you neglecting spiritually out of laziness, complacency, or ease? Do you do any spiritual activity that lacks connection with the Spirit? Is there some way you're serving God but in your own flesh or power?

The only way to give Jesus what remains in your life is to tie what you think, what you say, and what you do to the Holy Spirit. He will produce outcomes that result from His power in you. Without the Spirit's involvement, anything you do—even if it's done for God—is lacking. In Revelation 3:2, Jesus' message to the church in Sardis goes on to say, "I have not found your deeds completed in the sight of My God." Even though the church did a lot, Jesus found them lacking.

THREE STEPS FOR CONNECTING WITH THE SPIRIT

In Revelation 3:3, Jesus' message then goes on with "Remember what you have received and heard; and keep it, and repent." For the Christians at Sardis to really connect—or reconnect—with God's

Spirit and give God what He desired, Jesus instructed them to do three things: remember what they had already received, keep (act on) what they had received, and repent. And for us to connect with God's Spirit, we need to do the same things.

1. Remember What You Already Know

When Jesus asks the Sardis Christians to remember what they've already heard, He's referring to the biblical teaching given to them by the apostles. They weren't applying what they'd heard, but they had enough Bible knowledge and small-group participation to know how to do what they weren't doing.

Sometimes we don't need new sermons. We just need to do something with the old sermons that gave us biblical instructions we've not yet acted upon. Because if all we're doing is digesting information rather than implementing what we've learned from it, we're not fully experiencing the Christian life.

This reminds me of the story about a pastor who, on the first Sunday of the month, preached that everyone must be born again. The second Sunday he again preached that everyone must be born again. And the third Sunday, he once again preached that everyone must be born again. After hearing the same message for three consecutive weeks, a deacon asked the pastor why he kept preaching the same thing.

The pastor said, "Because we must all be born again!"

The deacon understood what the pastor meant. Without the church members allowing God to do that one thing—give them a new life in Christ—anything else they did wouldn't matter. And so the pastor chose to focus on what mattered most for as long as necessary. He wanted to emphasize that before moving on to more, his congregation needed to remember what they'd been taught up to that point. In other words, they needed to remember what they already knew to do. And so do we.

2. Act on What You Already Know

We each need to be personally responsible to act on what we already know to do, because the Holy Spirit and the electric current from Him flows only in the context of motion. The Spirit responds to our *walking according to the Word*, not merely *talking about the Word*. This is the second thing the church in Sardis was called to do in Jesus' message—put into action what they remembered of God's Word. And again, this is a call for us as well. James 1:22 says, "Prove yourselves doers of the word, and not merely hearers," and in Luke 11:28, Jesus said, "Blessed are those who hear the word of God and keep it!" (NKJV).

3. Repent

Then the Christians in Laodicea were told to repent. To repent means to turn from what you're doing that the Word says not to do and then start doing what it says to do. This is turning away from something while simultaneously turning toward something else. It's not merely a word you say or a prayer you pray. The church in Sardis was called upon to repent from turning their back on God. They were to repent from knowing what to do but failing to do it out of laziness and complacency. They were to turn from their own selfish desires and attitudes while turning toward God, remembering His kingdom worldview, and putting it into practice.

And what would happen if the church in Sardis did not repent? Jesus said, "If you do not wake up, I will come like a thief, and you will not know at what hour I will come to you" (verse 3). Remember, that's what happened to the city of Sardis when the armies of Cyrus and Antilogous came during the night with a surprise attack. The Christians in Sardis knew that history.

THE SPIRIT-FILLED, SPIRIT-LED WALK

And then Jesus' message said, "You have a few people in Sardis who have not soiled their garments; and they will walk with Me in white, for they are worthy. He who overcomes will thus be clothed in white garments; and I will not erase his name from the book of life, and I will confess his name before My Father and before His angels" (verses 4-6).

God was using a few people in the church to advance His kingdom rule on earth. They weren't the majority; they were a remnant. But He didn't overlook them. He didn't skip them. He noticed the few who had chosen to put Him first, and He mentioned them in the context of garments. To soil a garment indicated a stain from something in the world, whether from food or dirt or anything else.

But James 1:27 tells us we are to keep ourselves unstained by the world. Thus, God pointed out that the remnant at Sardis had not given in to worldliness. They had not given in to the world's viewpoint and perspective. They had not merged the world's wisdom with God's.

Let's look at three ways this remnant in Sardis shows what living a Spirit-filled, Spirit-led life is like.

1. Committing Ourselves to Christ's Ways, Not Culture's Ways

To put it another way, the remnant had not tried to accommodate the culture. They'd stayed committed to Christ. They had not chosen to compromise with the culture instead of living in commitment to Christ within it. As I've mentioned in previous chapters, far too many believers today so want to be acceptable to the world that they compromise their Christian values. They do this so they can be liked or followed or make progress in some other unimportant way.

This compromising for the culture is why we don't read anything about persecution for the members of the church in Sardis. The remnant was apparently small enough that they had not drawn attention to the point of persecution. In fact, most people in Sardis were applauding the church there. Even the pagans spoke highly of them, most likely because they had become so secularized, culturized, and as a result, popular. In short, they had given in to worldliness.

2. Striving for Godliness, Not Worldliness

Worldliness is that system headed by Satan that leaves God out. When you've pushed God and Jesus to the sidelines because you don't want to offend anyone or you're concerned about what they may say or think about you, you've just become worldly. Worldliness isn't only about partying in the fast lane. Worldliness is anything you take part in that leaves God out as the primary determining worldview for how the things of this world should be experienced. "Soiling your garments" is done anytime you place another viewpoint or perspective higher than God's.

It's easy to judge certain overt sins because our Christian culture has taught us to identify them and call them out. But complacency due to ease is a sin that warrants God's strictest judgments. A close look at why God destroyed Sodom and Gomorrah reveals that boldly. To live for Christ involves much more than avoiding a certain list of do nots. It involves placing all of your life underneath the Lordship of Jesus Christ. All of your thoughts. All of your emotions. All of your words. All of your actions. When you do that, you will be called out as the remnant like the remnant in Sardis.

3. Keeping Our Reputation, Not Losing It

In verses 4 and 5, we see that because this remnant did not acquiesce to the culture, because they considered godliness over worldliness, Jesus said, "They will walk with Me in white for they are worthy. He who overcomes will thus be clothed in white garments." It's important to notice that He used the word *white* twice. He's talking about clothes because Sardis had a thriving garment district. In those days, a white garment would be similar to our tuxedo or ball gown today. White garments were formal wear for special occasions. They denoted a sense of the regal and authority. To put it in everyday language, Jesus was saying the overcomers in Sardis would be dressed to the nines.

Now, that begs the question, why would someone get dressed to the nines? Typically, only if they have somewhere to go looking like that. The white garments revealed a special invitation to God's formal affairs. Jesus is telling us that He's going to invite those who are willing to be fully committed to Him and don't play church to His special events. They'll receive an invitation to a variety of unique and specialized experiences in heaven. What's more, they will not have their name erased from the book of life.

Now, reading that passage may pose somewhat of a challenge since Scripture teaches eternal security (see Romans 8:38-39 as well as other passages). Eternal security means that once a person is truly saved, they're always saved. They can't lose their salvation based on anything they do or have done. So when Jesus refers to erasing a name from the book of life, He's referring back to when He first mentioned "name" to the Sardis church. He says they have a name, but they're dead. Spiritually dead. The word *name* in that context means reputation.

Biblical hermeneutics requires that we look at the context of a verse or passage and not just the verse or passage itself. Thus, based on this context, what will not be blotted out is the person's reputation. They will still be known in heaven for what they did on earth. They will be recognized eternally for their commitment. It will be like having your personal name on your own VIP parking spot.

This is important for most believers, because they don't make the front pages of the spiritual news. Few may know your name. Few may recognize you. You may have never received a plaque for serving God. But maybe you visit the sick or the homeless or the elderly. Maybe you're a behind-the-scenes person who makes sure everything gets done so that the work of the Lord can be carried out. Whatever the case, if that's you, when you get to heaven your reputation will have preceded you. What's more, it will remain with you. You will be recognized for being the prayer warrior you were, or the devoted parent you were, or the committed leader you were.

In heaven, there won't be a hierarchy of popularity like our culture here compels people to live by. You'll be known by your name, which is your reputation, when you live as an overcomer—a follower of Jesus Christ, empowered by your connection to the Holy Spirit.

In His message Jesus concludes in verse 5, "I will confess his name before My Father and before His angels." If you choose to live as an overcomer, Jesus will advertise you! He'll put you and your reputation on a billboard. He'll recognize what you've done for Him. Being an overcomer means overcoming subtle sins like complacency, ease, a desire for cultural popularity, and spiritual distance from the Holy Spirit. And you can overcome these when you stick close to Jesus and make His will and desire your own. As you do this, He will manifest His strength through you as the Spirit enables you to live out your life as His kingdom overcomer.

That's the Spirit-filled, Spirit-led walk Jesus wanted for the church in Sardis and wants for us today.

7

ACCESSING SPIRITUAL AUTHORITY

THE CHURCH IN PHILADELPHIA
(Revelation 3:7-13)

I do a lot of flying to speak at conferences or events, and I'm fascinated by the mechanics of an airplane and all that goes into keeping it airborne. Do you know how rare it is for an airplane to crash? They're sturdy and well designed to weather many potential challenges. But it's possible for an invisible, powerful wind shear to suddenly force a plane downward with such pressure that it's unable to recover.

Unfortunately, wind shears are difficult to detect. They seem to come from out of nowhere. But engineers have developed technology to stay ahead of danger. It's called Doppler radar. This meteorological marvel has the ability to see the unseeable, read it, and then let incoming pilots know what they have to contend with. Wise pilots pay close attention because they know radar can see and understand what they can't. They would be fools to trust their instincts and ignore the radar.

You and I can be flying along in life, minding our own business, doing the best we can, when suddenly something impacts us negatively. Some unexpected burst of opposition comes upon us trying to make us crash—or as many call it, have a meltdown. And we're also fools if we trust our instincts rather than trusting the One who can not only see the unseeable but help us make sense of whatever intends to take us down.

By now you should know that God wants you to be an overcomer. That you *are* an overcomer. Yet as we've seen in looking at the churches in Revelation so far, it's possible to be an overcomer in your status without experiencing overcoming in your standing. It's possible to be an overcomer in your position without actually overcoming as your practice. It's also possible to be an overcomer in your doctrine without living as an overcomer in your daily life. This is because a truth remains only a theory to you unless you put it into practice. And in order to put it into practice, you have to understand that unseen forces out there want to keep you from having a safe landing. They want you to crash.

But in His infinite wisdom and all-knowing power, God can keep you flying high and safe and ultimately enable you to reach your divine destination known as your calling. And in Jesus' message to the church in Philadelphia, we discover another key to living with earthly success in the midst of trials—tapping into kingdom authority.

WHAT PHILADELPHIA AND THE CHURCH THERE WERE LIKE

The city of Philadelphia was in an area known for earthquakes. In fact, in 17 BC a harrowing earthquake all but destroyed it. Rome came in as a result and rebuilt the city, giving it another opportunity at existence.

Philadelphia was not a wealthy church. Neither was it a powerful church. It wasn't even considered a significant church. They didn't have all that much going for them. Which is why Jesus begins His message to them with this reminder of who He is: "He who is holy, who is true, who has the key of David, who opens and no one will shut, and who shuts and no one opens, says this" (Revelation 3:7).

God was the One opening doors for them. God was the One guiding them safely through each path. The church in Philadelphia had learned to live in true dependence upon the Lord because they needed to. They didn't think too highly of themselves. They knew they were of "little power" and needed God's intervention. They had lived in light of their name, which meant "brotherly love."

In His message Jesus said to them, "Behold, I will cause those of the synagogue of Satan, who say that they are Jews and are not, but lie—I will make them come and bow down at your feet, and make them know that I have loved you" (Revelation 3:9). Scripture puts this concept another way in another place: "The LORD says to my Lord: 'Sit at My right hand until I make Your enemies a footstool for Your feet'" (Psalm 110:1). The point being, when you keep God's Word, even though you may have little power, little clout, little recognition, or even little significance by the world's standards, God will shift things, change things, reverse things, and move things so that even your enemies are beneath your feet.

You may not have personal authority, recognition, or anything else, but when you have access to Christ's keys of authority, His keys to kingdom power, you can accomplish anything He desires for you to do.

The interesting thing that significantly makes this particular church different from the others so far is that Jesus isn't talking about in the life to come when He says, "I will make them come and bow down at your feet, and make them know that I have loved you"; He's talking about earthly success. He references the Jews in the synagogue there in Philadelphia. Overcoming isn't only for eternity—although our rewards in eternity are important. Overcoming can happen on earth as well.

Living with an eternal perspective will lead to earthly success. God can open doors for you that will amaze you. You may not have the degree to get yourself through the door, nor the pedigree or even the resume, but a sold-out, committed, faithful follower of Jesus Christ holds the keys of authority that can access a level of influence on earth greater than any human skills or strategies could do. Not only will you be privy to the invisible attacks of the enemy—the wind shears aimed at taking you down—but you will be guided to and through doors that will take you further than you could have ever gone on your own.

PUTTING IN THE WORK

When you audit a course in college, you're saying you want the information without the responsibility. You want to learn whatever the course teaches but you don't want to bother with any assignments or exams. You don't want to put in the work. You just want the knowledge. Auditing college courses used to be a pretty big deal before the rise of online learning. When information wasn't at our fingertips, it came with somewhat of a cost in that someone would need to commit to, at minimum, attending a course in person.

But in today's world, learning is as easy as opening an app, streaming a video, or listening to an audiobook. In fact, information comes so quickly to us these days that many feel we're suffering from information overload. So we're also seeking to find better ways to sift through the wealth of information in order to make it useful rather than merely something we hoard.

While auditing a course or learning online can be helpful to your overall growth and development, it's not a wise way to approach your Christian life. You can't audit the spiritual life. Yet many people come to church to hear the Word and be inspired by the Word but make no plans to do any of the work the Christian life requires.

They don't want to incur any of the responsibility. They want only the benefits of the knowledge.

But whenever you audit a course in college, you need to know that you won't get credit because you didn't put in the required work. Similarly, if you merely audit the Christian life by attending church on Sunday in order to feel inspired, or you check off that item on your "spiritual" list but don't put in the work of personal and spiritual growth, you can't expect to receive the transforming power that enables you to live as an overcomer. Information without application has no transforming value. Not only that, but it lacks the authority that comes tied to the credit for having invested in the developmental process entirely.

JESUS OFFERS US KINGDOM AUTHORITY

When Jesus introduces Himself to the church in Philadelphia, He refers to a key. Let's read it again: "He who is holy, who is true, who has the key of David, who opens and no one will shut, and who shuts and no one opens" (Revelation 3:7). Now, when the Bible speaks of keys, it speaks of two things: access and authority. And when Jesus claims access to any door and authority over every door, He's letting the church know He holds the master key. In fact, *He* is the Master key. As I explained in a previous chapter, a master key is a unique key that locks or unlocks all the doors in a given space. Jesus is letting the church know He controls the kingdom because He has and is the Master key.

To put it in everyday language, He tells them He's in charge. He runs the show.

We read about Jesus' authority in another place in the Bible, and we've mentioned Matthew 28:18 before. Jesus says, "All authority has been given to Me in heaven and on earth." Then in Matthew 16:18-19, He lets His disciples know He's going to build His church, and when He does, He'll give the church the keys—plural—to the king-dom of heaven. Keys denote more than power; they speak of ulti-mate authority. Thus, if Jesus has ultimate authority by possessing the Master key as well as the keys to the kingdom, then we, His chil-dren, also have access to this ultimate authority when our lives are aligned underneath Him.

To put it another way, if you choose to skip Christ's way of get-ting things done and instead adopt your own or some other way, you're picking up the wrong keys. The wrong keys will never open or unlock the doors of the kingdom. If you want kingdom access to God's rule on earth, then you need to use keys consistent with His will and His way. God wants to rule not only in heaven but also in history through the person of Jesus Christ. That's why Christ holds all the keys.

We aren't seeing more of the Master key's power to overcome in believer's lives because too many people rely on the wrong keys. They're relying on worldly wisdom or cultural keys to access heav-enly authority and results. But God's rule doesn't work like that. It's accessed only through His kingdom keys. And you want to access His rule, because when you do, people no longer have the last say. They no longer have the final authority over you. They no longer push you into that corner or this corner or leave you out of the spaces where you truly belong.

Far too often we're shook up and bothered over the wrong things. We believe people have the ultimate power to open the door or close the door on our hopes and dreams. We believe people have the power to raise us up or put us down. We've somehow been misled to believe that people have the power to promote us or withhold the promo-tion we feel we deserve.

But people don't actually have that power—not legitimately, at least. Only if we *let* them have that power can they prevent us from living out God's divine design for our lives. We let them when we choose to use the wrong set of keys. Yet when we live our lives aligned underneath the Lordship of Jesus Christ—using His kingdom keys—we access His kingdom authority that overpowers and overrules all.

The church in Philadelphia came to understand this type of power and authority firsthand.

As we said earlier, they had little visible worldly power. But in His message to them, Jesus goes on to say, "I know your deeds. Behold, I have put before you an open door which no one can shut, because you have a little power, and have kept My Word, and have not denied My name" (verse 8).

Christ lets them know He knows who they are even though hardly anyone else does. He sees them even though they're entirely overlooked in society. He recognizes their lack of power, influence, credibility, and social status even though the culture largely ignores them. But because they have remained faithful to Him despite their lack of public prominence or upward mobility, He seeks to reward them with what they need the most—kingdom authority.

Jesus rewarded them because they obeyed Him and didn't deny His name. As we've mentioned before, at the name of Jesus is when every person will one day bow (Philippians 2:10). So He's not referring to most people's generic reference to God, because when the members of the Philadelphia church did not deny Jesus' name, they specifically did not deny the name of Jesus Christ. As a result, Jesus said He would intervene in their circumstances, overruling that which sought to rule over them.

If you've never seen Jesus intervene in your circumstances to overturn, reverse, redeem, or raise up what looked impossible to you, then you haven't yet experienced the authority of Christ. Especially if you've never experienced this at a time when you particularly felt you had little power. To witness Jesus come through for you when you don't possess the worldly ability, resume, or power to come through for yourself is what overcoming truly means.

Jesus doesn't need you to jump through the hoops culture sets up. If and when you live a life of obedience to Him, in abiding fellowship with Him, He opens doors for you that you could never open yourself. In fact, when Jesus is the one making the way, many people will wonder how you ever got to the point where you are. Because from a human standpoint, there is no way you could have made it there.

That is what Jesus assures the church in Philadelphia He will do—be the One to right their wrongs, lift them above the ashes, and open the doors for them to live out their destinies. He will raise them above those society says are the most powerful, and in doing so He will demonstrate His true power and authority over all. Not only that, but He will lift those who acknowledge He is the Source of their everything to serve Him. In that way, they won't have the option of thinking they did it themselves. After all, pride comes before the fall.

ADOPT HUMILITY

Nothing keeps you further from God's purpose for your life than pride. And while it's good to live a blessed life in the Lord and He can provide you with all you need to be satisfied, if you allow those blessings to confuse you into thinking you are bigger than you are, you'll have let them go too far. Humility is a big deal to God.

Never view yourself outside of the supreme authority of God's hand and rule, because if and when you do, you will need to face the lesson of humility. Learning humility is never a fun lesson. It's not something you should actively seek. Rather, you can keep from having to learn it by applying the practice of living with humility now. Living with humility involves recognizing the true Source of all you have and all you're able to do. That source is God. Living with humility involves remembering that, even on your best day, you're a sinner saved by grace. As long as that truth is front and center in your worldview and emotional grid, you will position yourself to live a life marked by humility and gratitude.

When you live from that kingdom mindset, God is free to open doors for you that your education, money, career, or pedigree can't do on its own. God gives grace to the humble. He will lift you up as you continue to give Him the glory due His name. In fact, He will lift you up out of situations and circumstances that appear impossible to overcome.

That's what the church in Philadelphia was told, as we saw in verse 9. Let's read it one more time: "I will cause those of the synagogue of Satan, who say that they are Jews and are not, but lie—I will make them come and bow down at your feet, and make them know that I have loved you." These individuals who had made it their mission to follow Jesus fully were to be rewarded publicly. They were to be rewarded in such a way that even the false believers—those of the synagogue of Satan—would know the power they had in Christ. They would be lifted up to such a degree that those who hold clout in this world order could not be confused as to their standing and kingdom authority. Authority, when based in Jesus Christ, has nothing to do with worldly standards or even societal connections. It has everything to do with relationship—a relationship with Jesus Himself.

This reminds me of a story about a big dog and a little dog—a German Shepherd and a poodle. The two canines were both standing by a closed door when the German Shepherd came up with a contest of sorts. He turned to the poodle and said, "You're just a little dog. You can't do much. Look how short you are! I bet you can't even reach this door handle. You've even got a tiny bark. But let's see who can get this door open the quickest."

The poodle replied, "Okay, but you're a big dog. You should go first."

The German Shepherd began to paw and bite at the door handle, but he couldn't turn it. So then he jumped on the door and made a lot of commotion. That didn't work either, so he gripped the handle with his teeth. Eventually, he got the door open. It took him nearly three minutes, but he did it! Then pulling the door shut again, he turned to the poodle and said, "Beat that, little dog."

The poodle walked confidently and calmly up to the door, gave a small bark, and then barely scratched the door's surface. A man inside, his owner, opened the door right away, and the poodle won paws down.

See, when you know who's on the inside, you don't have to go through all of that struggling. If you know who has the power to open the door, and you're close to that person, all you have to do is knock. And when that person is Jesus, you should never measure yourself by your size in society's eyes. Always measure your strength and power by how close you are to the Savior. The closer you are to Christ, the greater your access to the kingdom authority He has to enable you to overcome and rise up to live out your divine plan. Jesus can open the doors even the big dogs can't help you with.

The church in Philadelphia got to experience this firsthand.

THE REWARDS ARE MANY

The Philadelphia church's rewards for their faithfulness included:

Being lifted above those who held culture's rule in their grips. Again, Jesus told them, "I will cause those of the synagogue of Satan, who say that they are Jews and are not, but lie—I will make them come and bow down at your feet, and make them know that I have loved you."

Receiving strength for tough times—an extra measure of grace for the trials of life. That's good, because things were about to get real. And a quick glance around our nation and world today reveals warning signs that things are about to get real here too—if they haven't already for so many of us!

Being spared the worst of it. In verse 10, Jesus is saying, "I also will keep you from the hour of testing, that hour which is about to come upon the whole world, to test those who dwell on the earth." So while the world was turning upside down and tests and trials had become the norm, members of the Philadelphia church could take courage.

Let's unpack this last one a little more. They would not have to walk through the hour of testing alone. They would not have to navigate the difficulties and confusion on their own. While so many would be trapped by the scenarios of Satan at play, this church would find a way through it all. This is because the One who holds the keys is able to reverse the irreversible. He can flip the unflippable. He can even make enemies into footstools (Luke 20:43).

Nothing makes God more real to you than when He gives you a way out of what seemed to have no way out. Watching Him show up when all hope seems to be gone is one of the greatest experiences you can have. That's how you know He's helping you overcome. It's when He gives you the strength you didn't even know you had.

DON'T GIVE UP

But Jesus does ask you to do one thing, and we read what it is in verse 11: "Hold fast what you have." You are to not give up. When things look tough and all hell breaks loose around you, that's when you need to hang on even more than before. Jesus is coming, and in this same verse He also says He's coming quickly. But until He does, hold fast to the hope you have within. Hold fast to the faith you have in Him. Hold fast so that you don't throw in the towel just short of the victory He has in store.

When God is silent, He isn't still. You may not see Him doing anything, and it might seem like you're just waiting for nothing at all. But hold fast. Because when God shows up to reverse your situation, He will do it suddenly. In an instant. He often likes to break in to transform a situation or a relationship when you least expect it. He likes to show up when you didn't think there was any way your circumstances could get better. He often appears at just the right time when you think your trial will never end.

One of the reasons He does this is so there's no debate as to who caused this transformation. It'll be inextricably clear that it was heaven invading history in order for God to get the glory He rightly deserves.

Another reason is that God wants to blow your mind. He wants to surprise you. He wants to make you say, "Wow!" That's why, again, He will often show up and turn things around suddenly. That's why so many verses in Scripture encourage us to wait. We're told to wait on the Lord with faith and anticipation. He will show up when the time is right and overturn whatever you feel is over-powering you if you live your life according to His kingdom principles and values.

Once you own this perspective and make it the normative way you operate, you can live free from worry and strife. You can live free from fear of what other people might say, do, or create in order to keep you from your purpose and destiny. You can be free from all of that, because you know who's truly running this show.

You can know that even though people may look like they have power, it is Christ who has authority. Humanity doesn't get the final word in your life. People do not get to control you. You are free, because Christ, the Master key, holds the Master key. And as long as you stick close to Him in a spirit of relational humility and obedience, you have access to His authority, which can overturn and over-rule whatever you're facing.

I understand that the devil may be breathing down your neck. I know what it feels like to have Satan place an obstacle or painful scenario in your path time and time again until you simply want to give up. But regardless of what you face, if you will remember to keep your eyes fixed on Christ, holding fast to the faith you have in Him, you will make it through. Not only that, but you will overcome whatever seeks to hold you back.

GOD'S SPECIAL REWARD

In chapter 2, we talked about an overcomer's priority—placing God first in their life. And in that same chapter, we talked about how God hasn't moved when our relationship with Him isn't what it's supposed to be—we have. But did you know God can grant special proximity to Him?

The church in Philadelphia experienced God's hand of power in their lives, and so can you. In verse 12 they were told, "He who overcomes, I will make him a pillar in the temple of My God. He will not go out from it anymore; and I will write on him the name of My God, and the name of the city of My God, the new Jerusalem, which comes down out of heaven from My God, and My new name."

To be a pillar in the temple of God is to be part of a foundational structure of God's church. In Galatians 2:9, Paul calls Peter, James, and John pillars of the church. Their work and teaching held up the church so that those who came after them would have something to build on. In other words, those who overcome the propensity to give up would be rewarded with special proximity to God. They would become solid additions within His house. In addition, they would be given a unique, special name. This name would indicate prominence in the new Jerusalem, because not everyone is equal in heaven. Your position in heaven depends on your obedience on earth.

You can have a 40-watt bulb, a 60-watt bulb, a 75-watt bulb, and a 100-watt bulb. While all of them are bulbs and give off light, they don't all have the same capacity. A 40-watt bulb can't give you a 100-watt bulb's amount of light, because it's not set up to produce that. Similarly, all Christians will enter heaven through faith in Christ alone, but not all Christians will share the same wattage once there. They will not all have the same experience, because they won't all have the same relationship with Jesus. Jesus isn't deeply committed to many Christians in a practical way simply because they're not deeply connected to Him relationally (John 2:23-25).

Jesus wants to know that you're all in, that you're a full-time fol-lower, not a part-time saint. He wants to know that you'll not deny Him, nor will you disobey what He commands of you. Those who have fully committed their lives to Christ are the ones who will receive the gift of this special, unique name and all that it provides.

Again, trusting in Jesus Christ for your salvation will get you into heaven. But living your life as a fully invested kingdom disciple will allow your experience in heaven to be all you could ever hope for. What you do while on earth, accessing the keys to kingdom author-ity available to you, will impact your experience of eternity.

So as you seek to overcome the various trials and tests Satan throws at you, keep your eyes on Christ. Keep your perspective on His kingdom agenda. As you do, you'll not only gain access to spiri-tual authority on earth but also kingdom reward in heaven.

8

REFLECTING AUTHENTIC CHRISTIANITY

THE CHURCH IN LAODICEA
(Revelation 3:14-22)

N ow we come to our final church in the series of churches Jesus sent a message to as recorded in the book of Revelation: the church in Laodicea.

If Philadelphia was the church whose members accessed God's kingdom authority through their faith, commitment, and obedience, then Laodicea was the exact opposite. This church can best be described as an inauthentic church comprising people who are in it for themselves. They obey when it brings them glory, but they just as quickly turn their backs on God when it doesn't.

To say that Jesus is disappointed with the church there would be a gross understatement. This neither hot nor cold church, made up of lukewarm members, makes our Lord want to vomit, not just shrug His shoulders or turn His head in sadness. This church makes Him want to "spew" them right out of His mouth. And He can't swallow either, because He can't even stomach them. That's a significant reaction to their behavior.

After Jesus says in His message to them, "I know your deeds, that you are neither cold nor hot; I wish that you were cold or hot. So because you are lukewarm, and neither hot nor cold, I will spit you out of My mouth" (verse 15), we learn why He feels this way—and what He advises as a result—in verses 17 and 18:

> Because you say, "I am rich, and have become wealthy, and have need of nothing," and you do not know that you are wretched and miserable and poor and blind and naked, I advise you to buy from Me gold refined by fire so that you may become rich, and white garments so that you may clothe yourself, and that the shame of your nakedness will not be revealed; and eye salve to anoint your eyes so that you may see.

Laodicea was a wealthy community. There was a banking industry there, sort of like the equivalent of our Wall Street, a comparison we also made for Ephesus. It had a medical center, businesses, and everything else to give the illusion of security and success. Yet the kingdom of God isn't dependent upon the kingdom of men. Earthly success and wealth don't mean much to God and His standards. While there's nothing wrong with achieving success in business as long as we don't translate that success into independence from God in the church, it's not a direct correlation to spiritual success.

As I said before, oftentimes the problem with earthly success—whether it's financial, status, relational, career, or anything else—is that the higher you go up the ladder, the more independent you can become. And this can lead individuals to assume they know more than they do. They assume they no longer need to depend on God and His leading in their lives. Yet when your own thoughts become the *amen* that solidifies what you believe in the church, rather than God's thoughts, something tragically erroneous is going on.

Let's look at several ways of living Jesus adversely reacted to as He considered the church in Laodicea.

LIVING A FAKE LIFE

Of all the churches we've looked at in these pages, Laodicea may reflect American culture most closely. With all of our progress and all of our programs and all of our megachurches, we far too often wear only a façade of what it means to be a Christian authentically committed to Jesus Christ. The church in Laodicea has the right externals—they look good, speak well, and raise their hands in worship. But they have the wrong internal motivation, conviction, and authenticity. Wealth flows, clothing is made, and hospitals thrive with the latest techniques and advances in medicine, but true spirituality languishes in the background of so-called more important material pursuits.

Jesus knew all of this, and what He knew made His stomach sick. The main problem is that this church has become ingrown. They're more focused on themselves than they are on the kingdom of God. They're more focused on turning a profit than on living as a prophetic voice in the midst of culture. They're using religion when it suits them, but only when it suits them. In a sense, they're using God Himself. They're asking Him, "What have You done for us lately?" rather than "What will You do through us for others?"

Jesus doesn't mince words about how this makes Him feel. Neither does He mince words about who they truly are. They are "wretched and miserable and poor and blind and naked." Although in the world their name is written in print for all to see, that's not the name God calls them.

I'm sure some of you, like me, have been to Universal Studios or a similar theme park where you can tour lots that appear to be actual city blocks. One time when I took my late wife, Lois, and our kids on a tour like this, we all marveled at how real everything looked. But when the tour guide turned a corner and took us around to the back of these streets, we could see nothing was there. The fronts of the buildings housed nothing inside. In fact, there were no buildings at all, just wooden façades painted to look real.

Some of the towns we toured that day were where filmmakers had created famous movies. But as sometimes is the case with a hamburger that's too well done on the outside, once we peered within, we discovered that everything was raw and underprepared. Nothing truly lived nor thrived on these fake city streets. It was all pretend.

Similarly, it's easy to create a spiritual camouflage that makes it seem like something deep is taking place, but God knows how to see through the façade. He can look within to discover nothing much is going on at all.

Laodicea was situated roughly 45 miles southeast of Philadelphia. In addition to being a wealth capital of the known world, it was a fashion hotspot. In New York, we would refer to this as the fashion district. It would be where the well-to-do went to purchase the latest trends and the most luxurious fabrics. This city known for finance, fashion, and pharmaceuticals had a tremendous reputation. It was the ideal place to land on anyone's bucket list for travel in those days.

That may be why when Jesus decides to address them through an angel, He begins by reminding them who He is: "The Amen, the faithful and true Witness, the Beginning of the creation of God" (Revelation 3:14). He wants them to know before He says anything else that He is the beginning of the creation they now enjoy. He is the initiator of all they feel they have produced or invented. He wishes to remind them that He doesn't really care what they have to say about a subject or how much knowledge they've acquired, because as the Creator, He already knows it all. His is the final word on all things.

In other words, He says, "Listen up. I'm talking now." Then He proceeds to lay into them about what He sees in their attitudes and actions. They are neither hot nor cold. They are neither one way or the other. They have found a happy medium where they can enjoy the benefits of both worlds, but their lukewarmness has also landed them in the murky middle known as tolerance—that is, acceptance of sin.

To understand why He was emphasizing this to them in this way, we have to look at Laodicea's unique location. On one side of Laodicea sat the city of Hierapolis. Hierapolis was akin to Hot Springs, Arkansas. The waters there naturally heated up and provided areas where people could enter them in order to gain healing and refreshment. This hot water, full of minerals needed in the body, then flowed down into Laodicea.

Yet on the other side of Laodicea was the city of Colossae. The apostle Paul wrote a letter to the church there, which later became the book of Colossians in the New Testament. Cold water came down from that mountainous region, flowing directly into Laodicea. Cold waters also offer healing properties to the human anatomy. Yet when the hot water from Hierapolis met the cold water from Colossae, it merged into a lukewarm temperature in Laodicea.

Jesus used this known geographical reality to express a spiritual truth operating at Laodicea Bible Fellowship. He pointed out that they had neither the healing powers of the hot water nor the healing powers of the cold water, and they were rather inconsequential now that they were lukewarm.

Another way to look at the benefits of hot and cold water is through the immediacy of thirst. On a hot summer day, most anyone can appreciate a nice glass of cold water. (If you're in Texas where I live, that cold water gets transformed into delicious, sweet tea.) Or on a cold winter day, you may want to turn that water into something hot—like one of my favorites, hot chocolate. Not many people order a glass of lukewarm sweet tea on a hot day or a cup of lukewarm "hot" chocolate on a cold day.

In fact, someone sipping a lukewarm drink will often make a face and say "It's not hot enough" or "It's not cold enough." Then they set it aside. Yet Jesus doesn't say He wants to set the Laodiceans aside. He says they make Him want to spit them out. In other words, He lets them know they're unacceptable. Their spiritually stagnant state of toggling somewhere between Christian commitment and worldly gain is unusable, unspiritual, and unacceptable.

Jesus even says hearing their praise songs makes Him want to regurgitate. Their sermons make Him want to puke. Their "amens" make Him want to spit them out. Their spiritual condition too closely reflects their geographical location, and as a result, they have succumbed to indifference and complacency.

LIVING A COMPLACENT LIFE

One of the ways the church at Laodicea becomes complacent is in their own assurance of great wealth. Because they're rich, they feel they have no need. They view themselves as self-reliant. Self-sufficient. They view their job as their source rather than acknowledging that the Creator of it all is their Source. As a result, they clock in at church for duty rather than to cultivate a relationship. They no longer feel as if they need the Lord, so they try to merely placate Him, giving the impression of religion without the content it should contain.

But money in the wallet is never an indicator of the bank account's size. In our culture today, we've also fallen into the false theology that indicates if you have stuff, you must be blessed. If you have the nicer job or nicer office or nicer home, God must have blessed you. When in actuality, stuff and money can frequently indicate a distance from God, not a closeness. It's possible to live a blessed financial life while being close to God, but it's often not the case. The more self-reliant a person feels they are, the less they realize how reliant on God they are. We are all reliant on God for every moment in time. We are reliant on Him for every heartbeat and every breath. Yet it's easier to forget this when good things come easy to us.

I was speaking at a recent event for our ministry when during our open question-and-answer time, one of the attendees asked an interesting question related to this. He was a starting quarterback for an NFL team, which made his question even more interesting to me. He asked how, in those seasons when life is good, we can maintain spiritual fervor and vibrancy as well as a desire to grow.

I immediately thought about how football teams who win major competitions like the Super Bowl most often fail to win again the following year. In our chapter about the church in Sardis, I said back-to-back championships rarely happen because success tends to breed complacency. The motivation that drives the players to put in the hard work and long hours necessary to win is often rooted in the desire to get there. Once they've reached that pinnacle, the hard work is tougher to put in.

Similarly, when things are going well for a believer, it can become more difficult to pursue spiritual growth. This is because what often drives spiritual growth is difficulty, trials, and challenges. As we seek to make sense of the challenges around us, we increase our awareness of our need to walk closely with God and remain humble in obedience to Him. Yet when the bank account is full and our lives are free from drama or health issues, our contentment with where we are can actually cause us to relax any efforts toward spiritual growth.

I answered this man's question twofold. First, I let him know that the spiritual life is ever-moving. It's never stagnant. Therefore, if you're not growing, you're backsliding. If you're not developing spiritually, you're losing ground. So because of this, contentment in growth should never be a thing, because like in football, giving up yardage is never a good thing.

Second, gratitude is also a motivator for growth. By being grateful for all you have and all that God has done for you, you can discover increased motivation to continue developing your spiritual muscles. Complacency lacks a spirit of gratefulness. Complacency speaks of entitlement. But a grateful heart will always compel a person to look for ways to express this gratitude to God, thus leading to greater spiritual growth.

LIVING A SPIRITUALLY BLIND LIFE

Jesus starts by reminding the members of the church in Laodicea that worldly success—for us, that can be building up a bank account, owning more cars than we need, wearing the best clothing, and so on—can camouflage the need for spiritual growth. In fact, He says worldly success often only means the person is an abysmal spiritual failure. Even though everyone else may think that person has made it or is a success, what matters most is what God thinks.

He doesn't concern Himself with bank accounts, couture clothes, or any of what the world tends to elevate. He doesn't measure a church's success by how many pews it fills or how hype their praise music may be. God looks at the level of authenticity when He measures the spiritual temperature of a church or a person. None of the rest matters.

One aspect of the pharmaceutical industry in Laodicea involved methods to improve eyesight. For the time period, they were well-versed in eyewear technology as well as eye salves. But Jesus said that although they could see things clearly with their expensive glasses and ointments, spiritually they were blind. None of what they thought they saw was real. They were living in a dream world, because they were unable to see what was truly going on. They were unable to see how messed up they and the world around them really were.

It's bad to be blind, but it's even worse to be blind and not know you're blind. It's bad to be naked, but it's even worse to be naked and not know you're naked. It's bad to be messed up, but it's even worse to be messed up and not know how messed up you really are. It's bad to be spiritually poor, but it's even worse to be spiritually poor and not know it. That is what Jesus sought to tell the Christians in Laodicea. They didn't realize how bad off they truly were.

According to mental health professionals, some mental illnesses are comparatively easy to treat. But a few are nearly impossible to treat because part of the illness is the person's lack of awareness that they're ill. They're unable to recognize they have a problem and so they project onto others. They blame them. Therapists say they have the most difficult time helping these patients to better mental health simply because awareness is part of the healing process.

The church in Laodicea was unaware that they had any issues at all. They thought they had all areas of their life under control and in working order, including their spiritual lives. That's why Jesus wanted to spew them out of His mouth. Talking to them rationally wouldn't help them. Giving them practical steps for spiritual growth wouldn't help them. When someone is unaware that they even need help, it's nearly impossible to help them.

As a teenager, I was a lifeguard at the beach. Part of that job involved helping people who had gone out in the deep farther than they should have. When I saw someone struggling and start to go under, I immediately swam out to pull them in. My response was immediate because I knew the faster I could get to them, the less they would resist. When a swimmer is going under entirely, their rational mind starts to shut down in exchange for raw survival instinct, and so they're often more difficult to save. They thrash around so violently that the lifeguard becomes at risk as well. Many people have lost their lives while trying to save someone who was beyond the point of realizing their only hope was to accept help and failed to respond to the help being offered.

The church in Laodicea had reached a point beyond knowing they needed spiritual help. They were already underwater, and Jesus knew all attempts to help them would no longer be recognized for what they were. That's why He went straight to the point with them. He didn't commend them for great things they did; He let them know where they stood. He let them know He didn't play spiritual games, and while the world may look at them and call them a spiritual success, He did not. He knew they lacked commitment, dedication, and true love for Him.

Church had turned into a show, not a place to worship God. They came for the performance of the choir, the performance of the preacher, the lure of the environment to be seen and satisfy the public. They were like a beautiful car on the showroom floor of a dealership—with no engine. They had the look, but they lacked the reality to back it up.

It's like the man who drives up to a gas station and asks an attendant to clean his windshield. When the attendant does, the man tells him he's done a bad job. But when the attendant cleans the windshield again, the driver still isn't satisfied. That's when the man's wife leans over, takes off his glasses, cleans them, and then puts them back on his face. The issue wasn't with the state of the windshield; the issue was with his dirty lenses.

Laodicea had become a place that enabled believers to wear smudged glasses but still blame others for getting it wrong. They were enabled to live lives of projection, where their own sin and mistakes were never addressed, pushing any issues off on someone else. They were lukewarm, content to live without any personal spiritual responsibility.

JESUS' ADVICE

Jesus' advice to this church was as straightforward as His condemnation. Let's look at that again:

> I advise you to buy from Me gold refined by fire so that
> you may become rich, and white garments so that you

may clothe yourself, and that the shame of your nakedness will not be revealed; and eye salve to anoint your eyes so that you may see (Revelation 3:18).

He advised them to buy gold from Him, buy white garments from Him to clothe their nakedness, and buy eye salve from Him so they could see what they needed to see. Essentially, He told them to not look to their own provisions in the areas of finance, fashion, and pharmaceuticals but rather to Him. He let them know that He was the only one who could truly give them what they needed. All the other stuff they'd accumulated from the world's ways and means was fake.

True wealth, beauty, and health are all rooted directly in God as the Source. Unless the spiritual is out front in each person's life and becomes the standard for every area of their life, they're living a fake life—the way of living we first explored in this chapter. And doesn't that remind you of our culture today? So much is fake that it's hard to know what's real anymore. We have fake lashes, fake food, fake décor—and worse, fake news, fake resumes, and fake values, just to name a few. In fact, many of our churches are fake in that they don't truly rest on the foundation of God's kingdom values and truth.

We live in a time of deep deception both individually and collectively, all while carrying out weekly church services in the name of our Savior. But in His message to the Laodiceans, Jesus is letting us know that unless the spiritual is acted upon as our standard for all else, we, like the people in the Laodicea church, are fake.

Do you know how a goldsmith can tell when the gold he's purifying is ready? When he can see his reflection in it. Similarly, until Jesus can see His reflection in us as His followers, we are carrying too many stains from the world that are contaminating the spirit within us.

That's why we need to be close to God's Word and close to people who value God's Word and will give us Christ's perspective if we lack it ourselves. We need to surround ourselves with what reinforces the

truth of God in all we do. Whether that's listening to podcasts or sermons or finding friends who truly know and study God's Word, we
need to prioritize the input of truth into our lives. Especially because
we live in a time of heightened and increased amounts of cultural
lies, it's become more and more difficult to discern what is real and
what is fake, what is true and what is a lie.

We need to heed the advice Jesus gave the church in Laodicea more
than ever. We need to "buy from" Christ with regard to our financial
stability, our health—even our clothing. We must start with Him in
all things, whether that's understanding politics, how we approach our
relationships, living a life of modesty and morality, or anything else.
Never base your beliefs on what the pundits are saying. Start with Christ,
because His is the standard by which we, as His followers, should operate.

Let's look at some other realities this message from Jesus teaches us.

WE NEED TO EXPECT THE LORD'S DISCIPLINE

Jesus explained to the Laodiceans, and also to us through His
message to them, that He reproves and disciplines those whom He
loves. If you feel like you're under spiritual discipline in any form,
remember Revelation 3:19, where Jesus says to the church in Laodicea, "Those whom I love, I reprove and discipline." God brings in
corrective measures whether they have to do with finances, health,
material well-being, or anything else.

God will also bring discipline into our life to get our attention.
Thus, if you're facing a situation you can't seem to overcome, ask yourself if it might be due to living too much like the church in Laodicea.
Have you become too self-sufficient in your day-to-day life? Have
you become so reliant on your bank account or career or relationships that God has been marginalized?

If so, you may be facing something you cannot overcome on your own
and so God is seeking to draw you back to Him. He allows this challenge

so you can discover your need for His hand in your life. Rather than forsake you altogether, God patiently disciplines you to draw you near Him. To teach you. To guide you. To remind you of what matters most.

Not long ago I filmed one of my Bible study videos in a junkyard, a location known as the "castle of junk" in Austin, Texas. I marveled as I walked through the mounds of all kinds of discarded items, which the owner had reconfigured into various formations in an effort to redeem some of what had been tossed. Visiting any junkyard should remind us where our stuff winds up. No matter how much we've paid for a watch, an outfit, a car, or some furniture, it will most likely wind up as junk someday. That's just the nature of stuff.

And that's why it's so important to have a correct view of stuff. You can appreciate it, just don't idolize it. Don't place it, or the acquiring of it, higher than your view of God. That's the definition of an idol. Anything that usurps God's rightful rule or prominence in your life is an idol. You don't need to bow down to it or chant something in its presence for it be an idol. Just value it higher than you value God, and you have your idol.

The church in Laodicea had made idols of many material things, very similar to what we have in our nation today. Yet that's a dangerous way to live, because this world and its physical commodities are all temporary. Nothing lasts forever; it can't due to the nature of our world. Wealth goes away. Clothes get torn or worn out. Even health deteriorates with time. That's why living with a spiritual perspective is so critical. A spiritual perspective enables you to view this world and all it contains through an eternal lens. An eternal perspective is essential to knowing how to manage the material stuff of this world order.

WE NEED TO UNDERSTAND THAT JESUS IS KNOCKING

Christians who are not all in for God and His kingdom agenda— those who just want a little religion to help offset their worldliness, like drinking a diet drink with a pizza—have made themselves both blind and deaf to God's voice. They've cut themselves off from Jesus' invitation to fellowship closely with Him. We see this in the next part of His message to this church (Revelation 3:20): "Behold I stand at the door and knock; if anyone hears My voice and opens the door, I will come in to him and will dine with him."

Jesus is standing at the door of our hearts knocking, hoping to come in. But He's not pounding on the door. He's not banging on it. This is a gentle knock you can easily miss if you're living a lukewarm Christian life. If you choose not to prioritize growing in your relationship with God, you may miss hearing His knock altogether.

Many of the problems Christians face come about because they're not listening for God's still, small voice or His gentle tap at their heart's door. They're too busy shopping or taking selfies. They're too busy posting about their lives and views on social media. They're too busy getting their praise on or showing others how spiritual they are. And too many churches have turned fellowship with Jesus into something few can experience, because, by and large, they've turned religion into entertainment or a societal status symbol. All the while Jesus stands knocking at their people's hearts.

He's not going to open the door on His own, even though He could if He wanted to. He knocks because He wants to fellowship with those who desire to fellowship with Him. He won't force His love or His presence on anyone. Jesus comes in by invitation only. People must first welcome Him, because He will not go where He's not wanted—whether in corporate church or an individual's life. If they don't want Him, by basis of free will, He will let them have their life without Him.

But anyone who hears His voice and opens the door will dine with Him. To dine typically implies fellowship. If you ask someone to have lunch with you, rarely is it because you merely want something to eat. Rather, the meal is the backdrop to fellowship. You plan to talk and spend time with this person while you're eating. When

Jesus says He will come in and dine with you, then, He's referring to intimate fellowship. He's referring to getting to know you and your getting to know Him on a greater level. It's not about the food; it's about the fellowship.

And this fellowship supplies what you need to overcome. As Jesus says to the church in Laodicea in verse 21, "He who overcomes, I will grant to him to sit down with Me on My throne, as I also overcame and sat down with My Father on His throne." Meaning he who overcomes spiritual death, just as Christ overcame physical death.

WE NEED TO OVERCOME SATAN'S SCHEMES

The church in Laodicea bore plenty of responsibility for their unacceptable living, but let's be clear: Satan had a part in their downfall. But no use blaming it all on Satan and his schemes. God won't buy that, and neither should we. We bear plenty of responsibility for our failings too.

The good news is that Jesus gives each of us the opportunity to overcome the devil's ploys just as He did. Satan tempted our Lord three times, the story recorded for us in Matthew 4:1-11. Satan tempts Jesus to turn stones into bread while He's hungry, to jump off the pinnacle of a building and call on the angels to catch Him, and then to worship him in exchange for all the kingdoms of the world. Jesus responds promptly in telling Satan to be gone, referencing the Word of God to refute him each time.

Not only that, but Satan sought to indirectly defeat Jesus on the cross. Before He was crucified, Jesus—fully God yet fully man—was physically tired and hungry as well as emotionally drained because of the betrayal of people, in particular Judas. Luke 22:3 says Satan entered Judas. But the Son still honored the Father in going to the cross despite having asked if there was any other way to accomplish God's will (Matthew 26:39).

Jesus overcame Satan and his tricks to overpower Him. He remained strong because He remained tied to the truth of the Word and His relationship to God and His will. You and I can similarly overcome Satan's schemes if and when we remain tied to the truth of God's Word and His presence in our lives. But we won't be able to overcome Satan through religion. You can't play at Christianity and get beyond the devil's schemes. Lukewarm spiritual choices will get you nowhere. Only when you're fully committed to Christ do you access His overcoming power in your life along with the authority and position of ruling alongside Him in His coming millennial kingdom.

Now, that doesn't mean you will ever be perfect, but it does mean that when you do sin, you will recognize what you've done as sin and repent. You won't just be acting the part of a follower of Jesus. You will be living it out in all you think, say, and do. That's the key to living as an overcomer, the foundation we laid in chapter 1. As I said then, tapping into God's provision through the power and person of His Son, Jesus Christ, is the key to being an overcomer—to being a victor, not a victim.

So stay close to Jesus, aligned underneath His rule and tethered to His Word. When you do this, you can truly overcome all the challenges you'll face.

PART THREE

CHOICES TO MAKE

To overcome all there is to overcome as Christians, we must make some clear, crucial choices. We've touched on several, but in the last part of this book, let's explore three of those choices in depth: choosing to access God's power against Satan, choosing to be a conqueror in all things, and perhaps most important of all, choosing to pursue godliness and grow in godliness. As you'll see, godliness is our assignment as Christians. The pursuit is the foundation of our walk with Jesus while on this earth, and growing in godliness is the path to abundant life in Christ.

Ready to choose your best for God in these areas? Let's get started.

OBTAINING POWER
FOR SPIRITUAL BATTLE

On a hot June day in 1963, Alabama governor George Wallace stood in front of a building at the University of Alabama with the goal to deny Black students the opportunity to attend college there. He stood tall. He stood strong. He stood determined. And he believed he would be the ultimate victor that day—and every day. We know this by the well-known statement he made at his inaugural address: "Segregation now, segregation tomorrow, segregation forever."

Now he stood in the secure authority of his position as governor. In the power of that role, he sought to entrench an illegitimate and historical inequity even deeper in our nation's veins.

Little would sway Wallace from his position that day—except for one man who held greater authority. When President John F. Kennedy heard what George Wallace was doing to illegitimately keep Black students from entering the college—even literally—he sent one hundred troops to Tuscaloosa. They were ordered to overrule what the governor claimed was legal. The president moved forward to overturn and overcome a standard of injustice that had taken root for far too long.

The governor possessed power. The governor oversaw a police force that could inflict great pain on thousands of people. But the governor did not possess the ultimate authority necessary to retain his stance on the legal front. In the end, Wallace had to step aside and let the students in, because someone overrode his claim.

The evil one has stood at the door of each of our lives on more than one occasion. He stands tall. He stands strong. He stands determined. And he wants nothing more than to keep you from entering and accessing all that the spiritual life rooted in Jesus Christ has to offer you. He knows that once you gain access to kingdom authority, and once you learn how it applies in your own life, you will be set free. You will be released to fully live out your destiny.

So Satan seeks to bully you into compliance. He seeks to deceive you into compliance. He seeks to lure you away from Jesus through distraction, entertainment, complacency, or wealth. We've read examples of the various ways the devil intimidates and oppresses followers of Jesus while studying how the Lord addressed the seven churches in the book of Revelation.

No one church of the seven fully represents any one nation or individual. In fact, we all pass through seasons of spiritual growth where we may resemble one of the churches more than the others. And then as time goes on, we may resemble a different one altogether. All seven examples were given to us for our instruction and learning so that we can become aware of and identify what we need to do in order to overcome.

Satan wants nothing more than to block God's purpose for you. He wants to stop God's preordained design for your life. He wants to keep you from ever experiencing the abundant Christian life. And to do so, he stands at the door of your existence to ensure that what has been written in your spiritual destiny is not lived out.

But as you know from the challenging content we've focused on concerning the churches in Revelation, the good news is that you can silence Satan. You can get the evil one to step aside and let you pass. To whatever degree the devil is bringing havoc into your life, God has come up with a legislative mechanism to keep him from blocking you from living in victory as an overcomer.

In Part Two of this book, we not only read about and examined the churches in the book of Revelation but were briefly introduced to how we can overcome by looking at Revelation 12. But now I want to take a deeper look at this passage, because what we find there is profound. It's the tipping point between living as an overcomer or living in a perpetual victim mentality. And it offers a startling statement about the war in heaven. In peeking behind the cosmic curtain as we read this chapter, we discover the angelic conflicts taking place in the heavenly realm and how they impact us down here.

As a reminder, Revelation 12 describes it like this:

There was war in heaven, Michael and his angels waging war with the dragon. The dragon and his angels waged war, and they were not strong enough, and there was no longer a place found for them in heaven. And the great dragon was thrown down, the serpent of old who is called the devil and Satan, who deceives the whole world; he was thrown down to the earth, and his angels were thrown down with him. Then I heard a loud voice in heaven, saying,

"Now the salvation, and the power, and the kingdom of our God and the authority of His Christ have come, for the accuser of our brethren has been thrown down, he who accuses them before our God day and night. And they overcame him because of the blood of the Lamb and because of the word of their testimony, and they did not love their life even when faced with death. For this reason, rejoice, O heavens and you who dwell in them. Woe to the earth and the sea, because the devil has come down to you, having great wrath, knowing that he has only a short time" (verses 7-12).

This passage, and the entire chapter if you read through it, gives great context to what I call the *clash of the kingdoms*. This is a spiritual battle between good and evil. Even before Adam fell in the garden through committing the first sin, Satan was kicked out of heaven and sent to earth. And since the fall, all hell has broken loose down here. Yet Satan still has access to the heavenly realm, and that's why a spiritual battle continues to take place. The dragon, also known as the devil, is our adversary, and he's free to create havoc on earth. He's also free to speak on that havoc based on the permission we give him with our unrighteous words and deeds.

And this is why to be an overcomer, we must choose to access power for spiritual battle—God's power.

FACED WITH SATAN'S DECEPTION

As we've seen throughout this book, Satan's goal is to prevent us from actualizing all that God has planned for our lives. One of the primary ways he does this is through deception. He makes it one of his main objectives to deceive everyone on earth. That's why there's so much confusion and misinformation everywhere. Satan has stirred the pot of deception and heated it to the point of boiling over. Everyone on earth is subject to this deception on a regular basis.

You and I are living in a day of mass deception. People are being tricked about their sexual identity. People are being tricked about their gender. They're being deceived about the basics of and definition for marriage. They're being deceived on how to best handle finances. If we were to be honest, we'd have to admit that we're all being deceived in many ways when it comes to Satan seeking to usurp

God's rightful rule in our lives. It may be easier to point out what seems like the obvious ways in others, but the more subtle forms of deception can wreak just as much harm in a person's life, if not more. Satan has deceived the whole world. Some in very transparent and easy-to-spot ways and others in ways we can't always readily discern.

Regardless, this world order is in the devil's clammy and crafty hands, and he runs it by deception. In fact, every man ought to be reminded of Satan's deception on a regular basis, because we all have what we call an Adam's apple. This is what we call the pronounced protrusion of the front of the thyroid cartilage around the larynx in a man's throat—a reference to the piece of fruit Adam shouldn't have swallowed. Thus, every time a man swallows, he ought to be reminded that he's been duped by the devil at some point or another.

Satan has done a clever job at deceiving everyone with the goal of preventing them from living as overcomers. His main job in our personal lives, families, churches, and communities is to block us from entering into the university of spiritual growth. This is his goal, because if he can strong-arm us or manipulate us or even accuse us enough times, he can illegitimately keep us from accessing all God has in store.

After all, Satan is the accuser, as, again, we see in Revelation 12:10: "Then I heard a loud voice in heaven, saying, 'Now the salvation, and the power, and the kingdom of our God and the authority of His Christ have come, for the accuser of our brethren has been thrown down, he who accuses them before our God day and night.'"

To accuse someone references a legal action, because *accusing* is a legal term. It has to do with a complainant in a lawsuit seeking to defeat someone legally. Yet not only is Satan seeking to defeat us legally, but he's seeking to defeat us before God Himself. He accuses each of us before God—night and day. He does this by seeking out a legislative wrong we commit that will not stand before a righteous and holy God. He believes that by doing this, he can block God from fulfilling what He has ordained for us. He seeks to replace our kingdom purpose with sickness, depression, addiction, and even untimely death. (And Satan's goal for non-Christians is to keep them from converting and becoming a believer in Jesus Christ.)

In short, Satan wants to keep Christians from living out God's plan and purpose for our lives during our time on earth. We've seen this by looking at the churches to whom Jesus sent messages in Revelation. We've seen the ways a person or church can become ensnared or deceived. And this helps us live with a greater awareness toward the enemy's schemes.

Yet despite all of Satan's attempts at deception and all of his bullying, oppressing, and even accusing, we have the ability to overcome. We have seen what we can do to overcome Satan or the circumstances thrust our way in an effort to block us or knock us down. And the greatest of the ways to overcome is found in this passage in Revelation 12. Verse 11 reminds us that we overcome by the "blood of the Lamb," then continuing reference to the brethren, "and because of the word of their testimony, and they did not love their life even when faced with death."

FACED WITH HARM—EVEN DEATH

As I said in chapter 1, in America, we don't often have to risk our lives for our faith. While there is increasing persecution and definite opposition to the Christian faith in many pockets of society today, rarely does someone lose their life for calling themselves a follower of Jesus. But that is not the case around the world.

Maged Shahata had been born into poverty, as would be the fate of his three children. A follower of Jesus in a nation of Islam, Maged had little hope or opportunity for a brighter future than he'd had in his past. Living as a religious minority in a nation that's close to 90 percent Islamic came with its own challenges—discrimination and oppression, to name two.

Maged longed for a better life than the one he had known for his children. And because of this, he'd chosen to take an even greater risk—seeking employment in an even more Islamic extremist nation than his own for better pay. Maged's risk had enabled his eldest daughter to enter college, something no one in his family had ever done.

Hani Messihah also loved his children—three boys and a girl. His devoted wife adored Hani's laughter in their home and often remarked how kind he was, that he was given to doling out hugs and kisses at will. She called him her angel. Hani was always good for telling a joke or bringing a smile to someone's face. But he was also a dedicated and responsible family man. Wanting to provide for his wife, Magda, and his four kids at a level he could never do in his own country, he moved to another one to give them the daily food and shelter they needed. Hani knew this other country came with great risk due to his faith, but he was willing to take that risk so that his children could eat and attend a good school.

Yousef Shoukry was a quiet, 24-year-old man said to have the pure heart of a child. He dreamed of one day getting married and starting his own family. A believer in Jesus Christ and from an impoverished town in Egypt, Yousef knew he had to venture elsewhere to make enough money for that dream to come true. So he decided to move to Libya and seek employment there. His mother begged him not to go, knowing the dangers that lie in wait for a Christian there. But Yousef believed he had no choice. He needed the income to one day offer his own children an opportunity to avoid being stuck, like he'd been, in such an oppressive, impoverished environment in Egypt.

Maged, Hani, and Yousef were men of great courage. They were kingdom men. They sought to better their homes and their families through their own personal sacrifice. Yet in the process, they were tested by something that cost them everything they had.

On February 15, 2015, Maged, Hani, Yousef, and 18 others knelt as captives on a beach along the southern Mediterranean coast in

Libya. Their captors, Islamic extremists, called them "people of the cross." That was the nature of their so-called crime. Twenty of the 21 would later be confirmed as Egyptian Coptic Christians. The twenty-first man was not a Christian nor an Egyptian at all. They say he was from Chad. His name was Ayairga.

As the Islamic extremists went down the row wielding a tool to cut off the kneeling believers' heads, each was demanded to recant their faith and claim loyalty to Allah in order to be spared. Kingdom man after kingdom man refused to recant, most mumbling the words *Ya Rabbi Yasou* (O My Lord Jesus) instead. Thus, each man lost his life for his faith. They fulfilled what Scripture writes about in Revelation 12.

The twenty-first man, who was not a Coptic Christian, was also demanded to pledge allegiance to Allah, the god of Islam. What is reported next ought to do more than send chills up your spine and bring a sigh of amazement from your mouth, as it did mine. It ought to challenge each one of us to reexamine our own lives and the level of the testimony we live of this faith we claim.

It's reported that because Ayairga had witnessed the immense faith and commitment of the 20 other men, when it came time for him to pledge allegiance to Allah, he looked down the line and then back up to his captors and stated, "Their God is my God." Ayairga spoke this knowing that doing so would cost him everything. Yet he spoke it boldly, and those words haunt me even as I write this chapter. This man had witnessed such powerful faith, dedication, and commitment in the lives of his fellow prisoners that he converted to Christ at the expense of his very own life. Whatever faith these other men had that allowed them to leave life with such strong committed dignity and hope was a faith, and a God, Ayairga could believe in.*

I write that the words haunt me because as I look out over our

---

* The story of Maged, Hani, and Yousef is adapted with permission from *Kingdom Citizen* by Tony Evans, Focus/Tyndale House Publishers, 2018.

collective body of Christ today, at those of us who call ourselves followers of Jesus—"people of the cross"—I wonder if anyone would be willing to give up their physical life in order to be saved by God because they'd witnessed our own commitment to *Ya Rabbi Yasou*. Would anyone see our lives and say in the face of imminent death, "Their God is my God"? I wonder. Or, rather, do those outside the church look at the contemporary church of Jesus in America today and find little more than a religious social club? Is it made up of people no different from the society we've been called to transform? In the end, would we just become another church like the ones in the book of Revelation who heard condemnation rather than commendation?

While the statistics on divorce are debatable based on whose study you read, few pastors will debate the reality that divorce happens at an alarming rate in our churches, as does spousal abuse, both physical and emotional. Similarly, pornography has laid claim to our men by the droves. Our entertainment and music frequently look no different than the world's. And less culturally obvious sins (but just as severe in God's eyes) such as materialism, greed, and gluttony rampage both our bodies and our billfolds, often receiving "likes" on social media rather than accountability to serve, give, or love someone else with that which God has given to us.*

Is anyone seeing our lives and our sacrifice and our dedication and saying, "Their God is my God"?

FACED WITH SELF-DESTRUCTION

We only have to look at the indicators within our own four walls and beneath our own steeples to recognize that far too many individuals, families, and churches are simply cannibalizing into self-destruction. We have been called to bear fruit, but what do you call

---

* We see mention of these sinful patterns in Matthew 6:19-20; Hebrews 13:5; Luke 12:15; Colossians 3:5; Proverbs 23:21; Ezekiel 16:49-50.

fruit that begins to eat itself? We call that "rotten fruit." Because of this, our society is overrun by the enemy's agenda of chaos and upheaval. Because of this, far too few believers actually know what it means to courageously live victorious lives as an overcomer.

And few if any looking on say "Their God is my God," because few if any witness radical life change, commitment, and sacrificial service to the glory of God. The principles of surrender and humility have been lost on us. Surrender means much more than giving up your life in the face of persecution. Surrender refers to giving up your will for God's will to be done. It means yielding your purpose for God's purpose to be lived out through you. Even Jesus had to face the principle of surrender in the garden of Gethsemane when He asked that God's will be done, not His own.

Yet far too many of us have become content to live as secret-agent Christians, a concept I first mentioned in chapter 1, unwilling to surrender even our conversations, careers, or contentment to God's overarching rule. As we've moved away from our biblical moorings—our Judeo framework and our kingdom perspective—hell has filled the gaps we've left behind. Chaos has filled the culture we are called to influence and impact.

TAKE UP YOUR CROSS

Statistics indicate that the average person picks up their phone more than fifteen hundred times during the course of a week. But Luke 9:23 calls us to pick up something much more important: "[Jesus] was saying to them all, 'If anyone wishes to come after Me, he must deny himself, and take up his cross daily and follow Me.'" We are to take up our cross daily, not just our smartphones. To take up your smartphone is to become influenced by it. Oftentimes, it will even get in the way of what you're doing or keep you preoccupied from engaging in life. In short, taking up your smartphone dominates your every moment.

To take up your cross is to do the same thing. It is to continually align your thinking underneath Christ's thinking. To check in with Him and to see what He's up to and where He is guiding you to go or what He is guiding you to say.

Now, of course, to take up your cross doesn't mean you're heading to Calvary to die on it. No, Jesus already died and paid for the sins of the entire world once and for all. Rather, to take up your cross indicates a willingness to lay down your life daily for God's glory and to accomplish His will. It involves a surrender to willingly become identified with Jesus Christ in your day-to-day activities, no matter what it costs you to do so. It means to love Jesus and His kingdom agenda more than you love your own life.

Jesus has a big fan club. But He has only a few who are willing to pick up their cross and daily follow Him. Too many people simply want to be associated with Jesus casually. They refuse to identify with Him verbally, publicly, and with their actions. But Jesus doesn't need more fans. He desires serious kingdom followers. He doesn't need convenient or cultural Christians. He desires biblical Christians. Living as a fan of Jesus doesn't give you the power required to overcome life's challenges—to fight spiritual battles. It's only when you pick up your cross—live in daily obedience to Jesus as Lord and Ruler over all—that you access the kingdom authority needed to overcome.

GOD'S POWER MANIFESTED IN OUR LIVES

If you ever need a passage to build your life around, if you want a pursuit to focus on for the rest of your life, Philippians 3:8-11 is a great one. It was written by the apostle Paul.

> I count all things to be loss in view of the surpassing value of knowing Christ Jesus my Lord, for whom I have suffered the loss of all things, and count them but rubbish so that

I may gain Christ, and may be found in Him, not having
a righteousness of my own derived from the Law, but that
which is through faith in Christ, the righteousness which
comes from God on the basis of faith, that I may know
Him and the power of His resurrection and the fellowship
of His sufferings, being conformed to His death; in order
that I may attain to the resurrection from the dead.

Let's look at several ways God's power is manifested in our lives,
as we see in this passage from Paul.

The Power of Resurrection

Paul speaks about a power beyond his own. He speaks about the
foundation for overcoming whatever life may throw at you.

Now, we know about resurrection power; it's the power that raised
Jesus up out of the grave. That's the level of power we can tap into. So
let me ask you this: What problem or need do you have that resurrection power can't handle? What is dead in your life that needs resurrection? Where does Satan have a hold—or relentlessly tries to take
one? When you make your connection with Christ your first priority, a key to overcoming we discussed in chapter 2, you gain access
to resurrection power in order to exercise kingdom authority so you
can prevail and be victorious over Satan's sin and circumstances.

Paul once made a very interesting statement in regard to his knowledge of Christ: "Even though we have known Christ according to
the flesh, yet now we know Him in this way no longer" (2 Corinthians 5:16). Before his conversion, Paul knew about Christ in the
sense that he had heard about this man called Jesus and perhaps had
even seen Him once. But after becoming a Christian, Paul came to
truly know the Lord, and his previous, casual knowledge was erased
because he became a brand-new creation (verse 17).

What happened to Paul was a genuine "power encounter." He

came face-to-face with resurrection power. When you know Christ, the old stuff is erased. No wonder the apostle said, in effect, "Out with the old knowledge. I've found the new!"

Why is it that some Christians have victory while others are defeated? The answer isn't in their circumstances, because victorious Christians and defeated Christians face basically the same kinds of trials. The answer isn't in who goes to church more often or who reads the Bible more. The answer is that victorious Christians know Christ more closely, align themselves under His rule more fully, and thus experience His resurrection power.

The Power of the Fellowship of Sufferings

A lot of us would like to put a period after the phrase *the power of His resurrection* in Paul's Philippians 3:10 declaration. We'd like to skip "and the fellowship of His sufferings" in the same verse. But if we're going to know Christ in the way He wants to be known—a way that draws us close to Him—we must know Him in "the fellowship of His sufferings," followed by "being conformed to His death."

We are called to share in Christ's sufferings, another meaning for carrying the cross of Christ daily. For most of us in America, that simply means standing up for Christ even when someone at work or anywhere else is making us feel uncomfortable because of our faith. For Paul, tough, fellowshipping with Christ in His sufferings meant severe persecution, numerous hardships, and finally martyrdom.

But it also meant a special kind of intimacy with the Lord that can't be known any other way. If you've ever suffered deeply alongside another person, you know what I'm talking about. We'll never be truly intimate with someone if we say to that person, "I only want to share the good times with you. Keep your suffering to yourself."

My late wife, Lois, and I were married for nearly 50 years before she transitioned to eternal Glory. When two people share their lives for that long, they come to know each other so well that they anticipate each other's thoughts. Many times we would say the same thing at the same time, or one of us would say just what the other was about to say. We joked about it, but it's part of the beauty of relational closeness. Jesus desires that we connect so closely with Him and know His heart and His Word so deeply that we think His thoughts and anticipate what He's about to say next in guiding, leading, or directing us.

The Power of Relationship

The power to overcome—to fight spiritual battles—comes from your connection to Jesus Christ, your relationship with Him. That's the bottom line. It comes from knowing the person of Christ and from receiving the righteousness and kingdom authority that comes only through your abiding relationship with Him.

In Philippians 3:10, Paul made his most desired outcome for his connection to Christ clear: "that I may know Him." So many Christians want to hear what five things they can do to live as overcomers or the four steps to victory over life's challenges. That's the American way: "Just give me a list of things to do, and I'll get right to it." But that's not what we've learned in studying the seven churches in Revelation. It's not about a list; it's about love. It's not about religion; it's about a relationship.

Now, nothing I'm saying about performance-based Christianity is meant to imply that we don't have to do anything as Christians. God has prepared us to do good works (Ephesians 2:10). And there may well be four or five things we could either stop doing or start doing to strengthen our walk with Christ. The problem is that we often attribute power to our *lists*.

Suppose someone says to me, "Tony, give me a list of five things I can do to live as an overcomer." So I give them a list of the basic stuff, like reading the Bible and spending time in prayer, and then I call them two weeks later to see how it's going.

"Not really any better," they tell me. "I already knew about the things on the list. I just can't seem to pull them off consistently."

This person's problem is our problem too. We know what to do. The issue is where we get the power to do what we know. The Bible says the power comes in the relationship. The power comes when the living Word, Jesus Christ, reaches the implanted word in our soul (James 1:19-21). This ongoing abiding with Jesus Christ allows the seed within us to be fed the spiritual nourishment of the Word of God.

And as it is fed, it grows. Through its growth, it begins to expand and dominate our souls. It is then that we find ourselves truly abiding in an overcoming power that is not our own. It is then that we find our thoughts reflecting God's thoughts, our hopes reflecting God's hopes, and our views reflecting God's views. Our lists are no longer lists, because we naturally gravitate to the things we used to have to force ourselves to do. This is because the Word implanted deep within us has received the living words from Jesus Christ on an ongoing basis as it is applied by our obedience. His power manifests itself in our lives.

The Power of a Revitalized Life

When Jesus died, we died with Him to the old fleshly way of life. But that's not the end of the story. When Christ got up out of the grave, we got up with Him! Paul said this was his goal in identifying with Christ: "in order that I may attain to the resurrection from the dead" (Philippians 3:11). That sounds like he was talking about the resurrection at the end of time. But there's more here, as great as that is. It doesn't show up in English translations, but there's a Greek prefix attached to the word *resurrection* that literally means "out of resurrection." Paul wanted to be resurrected out of something. What was it?

We could translate this as "the resurrection out from among the dead." Paul wanted to be so alive in Christ that when he walked among spiritually dead people who did not know God, the life of

Christ would be pulsating through him with such power that it would be clear to everyone else that he was really alive.

Take a look at another person in Scripture, for example—the disciple Peter. Why did even the shadow of Peter passing over sick people heal them (Acts 5:15), and why did his chains fall off in prison (Acts 12:7)? How was he able to praise God for the privilege of suffering for Christ (Acts 5:40-41)? Because Peter met Jesus in a new way at Pentecost (Acts 2). Peter knew Christ in the power of His resurrection and the fellowship of His sufferings—and he had a revitalized life.

The Power of Connection

When I was a young kid living in Baltimore, the fire department came around on Saturdays and opened the fire hydrant to bleed the line. The water gushed out, and we got our shorts on and played in the water. But I couldn't understand how all that water could come from that little pipe. So one day I asked my dad about it. He explained that the hydrant was connected to an underground pipe that led to a reservoir. As long as that connection was in place, plenty of water would come out of the pipe.

As with my nonworking refrigerator illustration earlier in this book, the one its new owner had failed to plug into an electrical outlet, if there's no water of life gushing out from you, enabling you to overcome life's difficulties, distractions, and disasters—some of which the devil likes to promote— you don't need a bigger pipe. You need to fix the connection. You need something inside that connects you with the power Source. You need a closer, tighter, and deeper relationship with the One who has what you need to overcome, because He Himself has overcome it all. Being under Jesus' authority, due to our intimate relationship with Him, puts us over Satan's power so that we are overcomers (Romans 16:20).

10

LIVING AS A CONQUEROR IN ALL THINGS

One of the realities of life is that it's rarely fair. In fact, life offers us a bittersweet existence. Some parts are sweet, noteworthy, and make us excited about being alive. But on the other side of the coin is the pain and anguish, disappointments and difficulties we experience. We sometimes cause these ourselves, and other times they're caused by others. Nevertheless, they always hurt.

But if anything ought to garrison our faith and strengthen our spiritual walk, it's those times when God shows up in the midst of the chaos and brings us through. Our view of Him is broadened in those seasons we can't handle on our own but God gives us all we need when we need it most. It's one thing to hear *God is a waymaker*, but it's another thing altogether to see Him make a way. It's one thing to hear *God is able*, but it's another thing altogether to see Him work things out. It's one thing to hear *Jesus can fix it*, but it's another thing altogether to see Him fix it.

No Scripture speaks on overcoming more poignantly or more directly and fundamentally than Romans 8:31-39. Every key principle we've been studying and exploring through these seven churches

in Revelation can be summed up in this seminal passage written by
the apostle Paul:

> What then shall we say to these things? If God is for us,
> who is against us? He who did not spare His own Son, but
> delivered Him over for us all, how will He not also with
> Him freely give us all things? Who will bring a charge
> against God's elect? God is the one who justifies; who is
> the one who condemns? Christ Jesus is He who died, yes,
> rather who was raised, who is at the right hand of God,
> who also intercedes for us. Who will separate us from the
> love of Christ? Will tribulation, or distress, or persecution,
> or famine, or nakedness, or peril, or sword? Just as it is
> written, "For Your sake we are being put to death all day
> long; we were considered as sheep to be slaughtered." But
> in all these things we overwhelmingly conquer through
> Him who loved us. For I am convinced that neither death,
> nor life, nor angels, nor principalities, nor things present,
> nor things to come, nor powers, nor height, nor depth,
> nor any other created thing, will be able to separate us
> from the love of God, which is in Christ Jesus our Lord.

I don't know about you, but just reading that passage gives me
the feeling of victory, the opportunity to overcome anything in life.
There is power in the Word to remind you that whatever you're facing, it doesn't have the last word. Whatever you're going through is
a created thing, meaning it did not exist on its own. Even if sin created it, it was still created. And since it is a created thing, it cannot
have the final say. This is because God is over all creation, and nothing exists apart from His rule over it.

This truth runs so deep that when Paul wrote this passage, he
emphasized it in a way that doesn't exist anywhere else in Scripture.

The Greek word used in verse 37, which we translate into "overwhelmingly conquer," is the only time it shows up. Paul wanted each of us to know that we are not merely conquering. Nor are we merely getting by. We are not to live under or just above our circumstances. Rather, we overwhelmingly conquer through Jesus Christ, who loves us. You're not supposed to just make it through a situation or overcome. You are to overwhelmingly overcome! In other words, you are to live as a victorious Christian and superconqueror in Christ.

SUPERHERO-LEVEL OVERCOMING

Now, to be a super-conqueror or to overwhelmingly overcome, there needs to be something to conquer or overcome. It's hard to win at basketball if you play by yourself. Sure, you may be undefeatable that way, but not in the true sense of the word *win*. When nothing is in your face seeking to resist you, block you, or drive you back, your win will not be sweet. A win by disqualification of the opponent is rarely sweet. But those wins you achieve through sweat and skill offer a sweetness that lasts forever.

For superhero-level overcoming, you need to understand your standing in Christ. You can see this when we go back a few verses in Romans 8: "The Spirit Himself testifies with our spirit that we are children of God, and if children, heirs also, heirs of God and fellow heirs with Christ, if indeed we suffer with Him so that we may also be glorified with Him" (verses 16-17).

In this passage, Paul raises a twofold relationship reality related to Christians and our connection with God through Christ. First, he indicates that we are children and heirs. But then he goes on to say that if and when we suffer with Jesus, through our verbal and visible identification with Him, we become coheirs. Those are two very different things. Simply being saved by Christ offers you an inheritance as an heir. But going through suffering for Christ, or in His name, makes you a "fellow heir" or a coheir with Him.

A coheir is much more than an heir. For example, someone can be their parent's son or daughter and be an heir, but if they have one or more siblings, they each won't necessarily get the same inheritance in that parent's will, making them all simply heirs.

But being a coheir is a whole other level of connection. A coheir automatically attaches you to that which the other heir has. This context, along with the verses following it, sets up one of the greatest verses in the Bible for life application: Romans 8:28. You may know it by memory already, but let's review it here: "We know that God causes all things to work together for good to those who love God, to those who are called according to His purpose."

Knowing how this verse follows a section of Scripture that details the many sufferings or groanings Christians can face helps shine a light on it. It reveals the depth of which God can work all things together for good. Verses 17 up through verse 28 talk about struggles. But Paul wants you, a child of God, to know that in the midst of the tears and pain life brings your way, God can work it all out for good if you love Him and live in the calling He has for you.

When your life is punctuated with an authentic love for Jesus Christ and a desire to pursue His purpose for you, He can take your pain, your problems, and your challenges and work them out for a good result as He uses them to conform us to His image (Romans 8:29). It's like when you bake a cake. You mix all of the ingredients together in order to create the batter. You don't eat the sugar by itself. You don't eat the butter by itself. You don't down a spoonful of baking powder by itself. Rather, you blend the ingredients all together— especially what would otherwise be bitter—so that it all works together for the good of the cake *and* those who will eat it!

Life often works in a similar fashion. Any circumstance, relationship, or challenge you face may be bitter on its own. It may not smell good on its own. It may look formless on its own. But when God is allowed to blend it all together, stir it all with His grace, and place it all under the fire of His Spirit's presence within you, He produces something good. God, in His cosmic blender, can take all the things that cause you stress, anxiety, worry, or pain and blend them together for your good and His glory. That is, when your life is committed to Him.

Unfortunately, this verse is often quoted and claimed for all believers without any clarification on its conditions. But to live as a coheir requires a condition. Being a Christian on its own isn't enough to claim the promise in this passage. To experience a life where God causes all things to work together for your good has conditions. It's not a blanket-statement verse that applies to everyone. For God to work all things out together for good means you're living a life full of love for Him and according to His purposes. When you do those two things, you will experience His hand mixing and blending all things together for good—the good and the bitter.

Let's look more at how, by the grace of God, we can choose to be conquerors.

LOVE GOD—AS HE LOVES YOU

To love God is more than feeling positive emotional feelings toward Him. While those feelings are good, that's not His definition of love. We find His definition in John 14:15, where Jesus says to His disciples—and to us—"If you love Me, you will keep My commandments."

The way you and I are to love God is through what we do. He's not interested in talk. He's not interested in empty promises. God knows our love is real when we choose to obey Him. Loving Him is a tangible, measurable concept, not merely an ethereal, emotional feeling in the moment. You love God when you do what He wants you to do even if, and especially if, you don't want to. And that can be tough.

It's easy to do what God wants you to do when you like it or would have done it anyhow. But when your obedience to God goes against your natural desires, that's when your love for Him is revealed. God "knew" Abraham loved Him when Abraham obeyed His command to take his son to the mountain to sacrifice him. That's when God provided the ram as a replacement for the sacrifice (Genesis 22:9-15). Just as in any earthly relationship, spiritual love for God is demonstrated through actions. You get to see the blending work of God causing all of the ingredients of your life work together for good only when you love Him.

Romans 8:28 is a cause-and-effect verse. You have a part to play in living as an overcomer. The way you play that part determines much of what you experience in life. Submitting or surrendering to God in the midst of your suffering and negative situations is what moves you from living as an heir to living as a coheir with Christ.

Far too many Christians are satisfied with living as an heir. They're satisfied in knowing that eternity is coming one day. But when you live as a coheir, you get more than eternity. You get to experience God's hand in your life on earth. You get to tap into His overcoming power and kingdom authority on earth. You also get access to greater rewards in heaven.

God longs to bring you into a fresh and new reality and experience of Him where He takes the divergent things that appear to have no interconnectedness in your life and mixes them together for good. He wants you to praise Him as you see Him produce something positive out of your pain. The provision of God's good supply becomes particularly visible in the midst of painful scenarios as they reveal His heart to us in ways we never imagined. In Romans 8:32, Paul boldly proclaims God's heart toward us: "He who did not spare His own Son, but delivered Him over for us all, how will He not also with Him freely give us all things?"

I love the word *freely* in that verse, because it reminds us that there is no charge. Freely means that the good God gives us comes out of our coheir relationship with Him. This free flow of grace shows up when God takes the good, the bad, and the ugly in your life and works it together for good. The good refers to the things you're proud of. The bad refers to the things you may regret. The ugly refers to the painful stuff that life itself, or others, may have done to you. All of these things mix together to produce a good or beneficial result when you fully love God.

One of the ways Jesus becomes the most real to you is when you're going through something hard. That's when He shows Himself to you in personal and meaningful ways you can't even explain at times. He can do this because a coheir relationship is established and rooted in love. He acts on your behalf when you need Him most because He loves you. Just like you would draw closer to someone you love in their times of pain and hurting and look for ways to help them or comfort them, Jesus does the same out of a heart of love for you. The deeper the pain, the closer you draw to Him and He draws to you.

It's in the context of suffering that Jesus reveals His heart to you the most. That's where His power and authority become yours and allow you to live as an overwhelmingly victorious, conquering, overcoming Christian.

LIVE ACCORDING TO GOD'S PURPOSES

God not only wants you to be victorious; He wants you to be super victorious. He wants what looked like it would destroy you to become insignificant in your life. In fact, He can even turn it into something you praise Him for, because you recognize the good He produced through it.

The Joseph of the Old Testament experienced a tremendous amount of pain and suffering at the hands of his brothers, who sold him into slavery in Egypt. But his perspective—his living according to God's purpose—allowed him to see the good God produced because of it. We hear Joseph's heart in Genesis 50:20, where he says to his brothers,

"You meant evil against me, but God meant it for good in order to bring about this present result, to preserve many people alive."

Joseph didn't enjoy the difficulties he faced or the years he languished in prison having been falsely accused by Potiphar's wife. He didn't celebrate them and call them his best years ever. But he did recognize the good they produced not only in his own life but in the lives of many who were now benefiting from the results of the pain, challenges, and problems he'd experienced.

Rest assured, whatever or whomever you're dealing with, it or they do not have the last say. No matter how big, mighty, powerful, or pushy it is or they are, Jesus Christ rules and reigns over all. He is positioned higher than all other rule, authority, dominion, and power.

For example, the president of the United States sits in the Oval Office at the White House, and what he decrees from this seat of power can impact us as Americans and even people around the world. This is because a US president has a powerful position above most of our power as citizens and in some cases above the power of other branches of our government. But if one man in one city can politically affect an entire country, or even the world, what do you think the King of kings and Lord of lords can do sitting on His throne far above *all other rule and authority*?

Whatever your enemy, opposition, circumstance, or challenge has to say is *a* word but not the final word. Your boss may have *a* word, but he doesn't have the final word. Your doctor may have *a* word, but he doesn't have the final word. Your finances may have *a* word, but they don't have the final word. Your emotions may have *a* word, but they don't have the final word.

ACCESS GOD'S KINGDOM AUTHORITY

In chapter 7 we talked about this topic in depth, but what living as an overcomer through your obedience to Jesus and love for Him produces in your life is access to kingdom authority. As a reminder, authority has to do with power, but authority does not simply mean power. Authority is the right to use the power you possess.

For example, referees are not the strongest men among all the men on a football field. In fact, they're usually older and slower than all the other men out there. Yet when a referee throws out a yellow flag on a player who's much faster or stronger, that player has to yield. The faster man has to slow down. The stronger man has to do what the referee says. This is because the referee has a greater power called authority, and authority overrules power.

Here's another example. You may be driving a bigger, more powerful vehicle than the cop car behind you, but when you see the red lights come on, you pull over. This is because your power is irrelevant in the face of authority.

If this didn't come through in the previous chapter on our need for power to fight spiritual battles, let me let you in on this: The devil is bigger than you. He is more powerful than you. He is more cunning than you. He is stronger than you. You can't overrule the devil with your own prowess or power, and I caution you not to try. When you are identified with Christ in a loving relationship with Him, however, you are reigning as a coheir with Him, and His authority overrides Satan's power in your life.

What Satan can do to you from an authority standpoint is similar only to what a man holding a gun on you can do. At first, you may feel afraid and at this man's mercy. Yet if someone pointed out that his gun has no bullets in it, he would no longer control your actions nor your emotions. That's the difference between power and authority. Jesus Christ holds the authority because He "disarmed" Satan (Colossians 2:15). Jesus Christ removed the bullets from Satan's gun. Satan still likes to play like a tough guy and try to intimidate everyone with his power, but ultimately, Jesus Christ has stripped him of his authority. Therefore, his power is only as strong as he can persuade you to believe it is. In and of itself, his power is not strong enough to overcome Christ's authority.

When Satan comes at you, remember that he has an unloaded gun. Of course, he's not going to tell you that. He wants you to think you're not going to make it, that you'll never overcome and will always be defeated. He wants you to think that since depression, or overspending, or overeating, or financial devastation, or some form of addiction, or anything else challenging is in your family history, you will always fall victim to it.

But Jesus wants you to know there are no bullets in that gun! Satan was disarmed at Calvary. He no longer has the last word, because Jesus Christ now sits high above all other rule and authority. And you and I are seated with Him, sharing in that authority when we are a coheir with Christ based on our relationship with Him.

PRAISE GOD

Am I saying you'll have no problems? No. I'm saying if you will love the Lord your God with all of your heart and commit your life to fulfilling His purposes, even though you have problems, Jesus will teach you how to walk on water rather than drown in it. He will situate you above your circumstances rather than under them. He will work all things together for your own good, the good of others, and His glory.

One way to bring this victory about even faster is to praise God. Not for the bad day, challenging circumstance, or heavy problem, but praise for God Himself. Joseph didn't praise God for the prison; he praised Him in the prison. You can praise God no matter what you're facing because it is not the last word. Praise Him because He is seated high above all other rule and authority, and by virtue of your relationship with Him, you are seated with Him and therefore have access to His rule and authority in your life (Ephesians 2:6).

This is why our focus on the churches in Revelation is so critical. The believers, as recorded in Revelation 12:10-11, overcame. They overcame Satan because they never lost sight that the very thing set out to bring hell into their lives did not have the last word. They never lost sight that Jesus has conquered Satan, granting them access to an authority higher than the devil's own.

BE SEATED WITH CHRIST

God wants you to know, through these examples and illustrations in Scripture, that Jesus has provided victory for you over your enemies and the enemy. Because Jesus Christ is seated above all rule and authority, you, too, are seated there with Him. In fact, in Ephesians 2:5-7 Paul states, "Even when we were dead in our transgressions, made us alive together with Christ (by grace you have been saved), and raised us up with Him, and seated us with Him in the heavenly places in Christ Jesus, so that in the ages to come He might show the surpassing riches of His grace in kindness toward us in Christ Jesus."

Not only does Jesus Christ have a chair in heaven but you have a chair there as well. You have been "seated…with Him" above all other rule and authority. You have been spiritually relocated, and, again, you can access that authority when you love Him and live according to His purpose for your life. You might be saying, *If I'm seated up there with Jesus, Tony, then why am I not experiencing victory right now?* The answer is simple. Because access to kingdom authority is tied to your relational authenticity with the Lord. It's also tied to your awareness of that authority and your position in Christ.

Far too many people simply don't know where they're seated spiritually. Physically, we're on earth. Yet spiritually, we're in heavenly places. The best way I know to illustrate this is through the common communication portal of Zoom. During the COVID-19 pandemic, Zoom was a useful tool. But even in the infancy of teleconferencing, it provided us with the ability to transcend space and location like never before. Through this means, I could be sitting in my office in Dallas and yet be entirely and coherently present in a board meeting for an organization in Chicago. This method provided the opportunity to be in dual locations at one time.

Likewise, you and I are physically positioned on earth yet we're also in heavenly places. Unless you realize that, however, and operate out of that mindset, you'll be confined to what earth has to offer. You must approach your life spiritually in order to attain spiritual authority as an overcomer. If all you see is what you see, then you will never see all there is to be seen. If your eyes are focused on the here and now, you will miss experiencing heaven's rule in history. Earth's seat doesn't give you authority. Only heaven has access to that authority, because that authority is tied to Jesus Christ.

When you learn how to function in connection with divine authority, it changes everything. It changes the intimidation factor that others may have over you. It changes your fear levels, worry, dread, and all else. In fact, when I know deep in my spirit that God has shown me something He's going to do or arrange, other people saying it isn't going to happen or that it can't happen doesn't bother me. What other people have to say becomes irrelevant when you function according to the authority of Jesus Christ. You can overcome it all!

Knowing this truth ought to change how you walk, talk, and function. It ought to change your whole approach to life when you realize the difference between power and authority.*

Jesus can release you to experience all you were created to live out. If you want to be victorious and live as an overcomer, look to Him. Hang with Him. Rest in Him. Learn from Him. Jesus is the answer to life's challenges and difficulties, because in Him you can

---

* The content in this chapter beginning with the paragraph "Rest assured, whatever or whomever you're dealing with" is adapted with permission from *The Power of the Cross* by Tony Evans, Moody Publishers, 2016.

overwhelmingly conquer all. He wants you to be victorious. He wants you to live the abundant life. He wants you to become a testimony for His work in and through you so others will want to know Him too. But the secret to living as an overcomer is your willingness to press through the painful situations while rooted and grounded in Christ.

REMEMBER GOD IS WITH YOU IN YOUR TROUBLES

One of the verses we read earlier has a key word that many people confuse to mean something else entirely. Romans 8:37 says, "In all these things we overwhelmingly conquer through Him who loved us." The key word in this passage is a small word. You may skip over it if you read too quickly. But I want you to consider the word *in*. Because far too many people brush over that word. Or they translate it to mean something different, such as "from." They want the verse to say, "From all these things" rather than "In all these things."

But the word is *in*. And here's the reason that's important. If you choose to spend your life seeking to avoid the challenges and difficulties that come your way, seeking to numb yourself from them, or even distract yourself from them, you will not experience the overcoming life. Jesus gives you His grace and authority in the trials and troubles you face. But that means you must face them. You can't deny them, entertain your way around them, or simply pretend they don't exist. Again, to overcome something, there must be something to overcome. You need to acknowledge it and then look to Jesus to walk you through it. Denying it or merely trying to cope through it will only prolong its negative effects in your life.

If you look to Jesus in the difficulties, you will find Him. In the middle of the things you face is when God dips His hand down and lifts you up. When Israel was going through the wilderness, that's when God dipped His hand down and provided them with manna to eat. He opened up the heavens and rained down cornflakes from above. The Israelites were not delivered *from* the wilderness; they were delivered *in* the wilderness. That's a critical distinction to make as you live the overcoming life.

In the midst of the mess of life itself is where you can witness God's divine hand of provision, comfort, and deliverance. He will often ultimately deliver a person from a challenging situation, but not always. Nor does Romans 8:37 promise that. But what God will do when you keep your heart and your eyes focused on Him is deliver you *in* the circumstances and challenges. He will meet you there. He will give you the peace that passes understanding. He will give you wisdom and insight to help you navigate the winding and rocky path you're on. And even though your difficult situation, career, relationship, or any other difficulty may not change or improve, you'll realize that you're more than a conqueror through Him who loves you and gave Himself for you.

You are not alone. In the midst of the pain and problems of this life, you are not alone. God is with you. He walks with you. And when your heart belongs to Him, He will supply what you need to live as an overcomer both now in present time and in eternity.

But though I want to encourage you, I don't want to paint an unreal picture of this life. God is not promising that the devil will leave you alone if you follow Him. He's not promising that if you love Him, people won't seek to oppress or block you. He's not promising you a life free from bumps or bruises or sprains. But He does want you to know that since He did not spare His only Son but delivered Him up for you, your victory is secure. No matter what you're going through or facing right now, you can overwhelmingly conquer as a super-overcomer in Jesus Christ.

11

PURSUING A GODLY LIFE

Roughly around my third year of seminary, I got a major paper back from my professor with a big fat *F* on it. My goal had been to make an *A*. In fact, during seminary, I tried to make sure every paper was done at the *A* level. I loved my study subjects, threw myself into them wholeheartedly, and paid attention to every detail. So when I got that *F* written in what appeared to be neon lights, the letter seemingly lifting off the paper when I picked it up, my heart sank. Not only had I missed the mark of an *A*, but I'd missed it by a long shot.

I stood there shocked, staring at my grade, trying to figure out how on earth this happened. That's when I noticed the writing under the *F*. It was a note from my professor: *Great paper, Tony. Wrong assignment.* I had done the wrong thing with a lot of effort. And a lot of effort aimed at the wrong thing gave me nothing more than a failing grade.

As we've seen through our look at the churches to whom Jesus sent messages in the book of Revelation, as well as when we've taken a general glance at Christian culture today, many believers both throughout history and in contemporary settings have missed the mark. They've made a lot of effort on the wrong assignment. We're working harder than ever, putting in more effort than ever, yet winding up with a failing grade. We're failing in our homes, families, careers, priorities, and even in many of our personal emotions.

Now, we aren't failing due to a lack of trying. We've taken multitasking to a whole new level the past decades. The reason so many individuals lack the ability to overcome what seeks to defeat them is that their focus is on the wrong assignment.

This was one of the primary issues the seven churches in Revelation had, and it's a primary issue for many of us today. Because the Christian life all boils down to what Scripture calls *the pursuit of godliness*. The apostle Paul told Timothy in particular to pursue godliness as well as righteousness, faith, love, and perseverance (1 Timothy 6:11). You and I have been saved for eternity so that we can develop and live out godly lives on earth.

WHAT GODLINESS IS AND WHAT IT IS NOT

Let me define godliness so we're all on the same page, understanding what our assignment actually is. Godliness is a lifestyle that's consistent, both desirous and functionally, with the reflection of God Himself. Godliness is the hallmark of the Christian life, and your personal spiritual power, contentment, and satisfaction.

A soul that lacks godliness is a hungry soul. It's a starving soul. This is because your soul was designed to reflect God. It was designed to align with God. When your mind, body, and soul are out of spiritual alignment with God, your soul is nutritionally deprived and malnourished. Within you has been placed a soul that longs for the Spirit of God to move within, in order for you to experience more of God's presence in you.

Far too often, people assume they must give up something in order to live a godly life. But the opposite is true. In pursuing a life of godliness, you gain everything your soul actually needs in order to thrive. In 1 Timothy 4:8, Paul explains the importance of godliness and the motivation for pursuing it: "Bodily discipline is only of little profit, but godliness is profitable for all things, since it holds promise for the present life and also for the life to come." Paul writes this to Timothy to remind him of the benefits of godliness. Godliness is not only valuable for the sweet by and by; it's also good for the nasty here and now. Godliness is critical for living the overcoming life.

Now let's look at what godliness is *not*, because that will help you better understand the concept. In 2 Timothy 3:1-5 we read:

> Realize this, that in the last days difficult times will come. For men will be lovers of self, lovers of money, boastful, arrogant, revilers, disobedient to parents, ungrateful, unholy, unloving, irreconcilable, malicious gossips, without self-control, brutal, haters of good, treacherous, reckless, conceited, lovers of pleasure rather than lovers of God, holding to a form of godliness, although they have denied its power; Avoid such men as these.

These descriptive terms help us recognize what is known in Scripture as a "form of godliness." A form of something is not the thing itself. It's something that resembles the thing and looks like the thing but is not the thing. The Greek word for "form" simply means "shape," or "silhouette." It's an appearance, outline, or even a shadow of the real thing, but it's not the real thing itself. When you see a shadow of a person, you're seeing the outline of their substance. In other words, the shadow is not the person at all. Thus, to live with a form of godliness is not living with godliness itself. It's living with something that reflects godliness, but when touched, felt, or examined, it falls short. It is, rather, an empty shadow holding no substance at all. And because it holds no substance, it also carries no power.

Anyone can dress up in a Superman or Avenger's costume to look the part, but that doesn't make them a superhero. If they tried to fly, they would fall. If they tried to carry out superhero powers, they would fail. If they tried to leap a building, they would simply run into a brick wall. That's because a costume is not the character itself. A form of something lacks the power necessary to carry out what the true person or thing contains.

One time I arrived at a hotel hungry, so naturally, I approached the table that had water and other welcome items sitting out. I grabbed an apple and took a bite only to discover it was wax. I'd stuck my teeth into a waxed apple! The apple wasn't real at all. It had the form of an apple, it had the color of an apple, and it had the look of an apple, but it did not have the substance of an apple. It had seemed so authentic, and yet its reality was not present and there was certainly no nutritional satisfaction in that bite.

This form of godliness the Bible refers to is also known as religion. Religion gives the impression of something related to God that is real, but it is not real. It's a form. A person can appear to be religious. They can wear religious clothes. They can use religious vocabulary. They can speak Christianese. They can even carry a Bible under their arm and hang out with other people who do the same thing. Yet regardless of all of these external actions, they have no true spiritual power. This is because spiritual power is tied to a relationship with Christ. It does not come from religion.

I've been a pastor for multiple decades, and like I'm sure you have, I've seen many people who have attended church for years yet see no real change or spiritual growth in their lives. They've put in the hours and logged the time, but spiritual growth doesn't come about through showing up. Spiritual maturity—also known as godliness—comes through intimacy with God. Going to church, in and of itself, does not have the power to make you more godly, just like going into a garage doesn't have the power to transform you into a car. The location is not sufficient for the purpose.

One of my favorite places is a donut shop less than a mile from my home. I've gone there for decades, and its owners are still the same ones. (As you might imagine, they know me by name.) Every donut in this shop is sweet. And they've all been sprinkled with sugar. If you want to make a donut taste really great, just stick it in a microwave for a few seconds. That makes the sugar run melting down its sides.

No matter how often we go to a donut shop, though, we're probably no better off for it. In fact, the more often we go, the worse off we probably are. Even though the environment is sweet. Even though the aroma is sweet. Even though they all look so great, there's no nutritional value in eating a donut. All you get are empty calories with no physical benefit.

For many people, the church is God's donut shop. They come to hear a sweet song. They want to hear a sweet sermon. They enjoy the sweet atmosphere and seeing everyone dressed up all sweet with their Sunday-sweet smiles. But when there is no true connection to the living God and it's all about the form of religion, they leave without any spiritual maturity at all. You can have the look without its reality. You can have the paraphernalia without power. You can have the form of spirituality without true kingdom authority.

Thus, if you're going through life without the spiritual power available to you as a child of the King, you have to ask yourself if you're pursuing godliness or simply living out a routine—the rituals—of Christianity.

True godliness rests in a right relationship with God. When you tap into that, you tap into true power. If you'll recall, in the Old Testament narrative of Moses and Pharaoh's magicians, the magicians threw down their sticks, and the sticks became snakes. They had the form of power. But when Moses threw down his rod, it also became a snake—that then ate up the magicians' snakes. This is because Moses' snake didn't only have the appearance of a snake; it had the power of a snake.

Only godliness comes with the power that enables you to be an overcomer. Godliness, therefore, is demonstrated by power. And so important is this aspect of the spiritual life that Scripture uses the term *godliness* over a dozen times in the New Testament. Most of these times show up in the epistles, letters written to the early churches. I would expect it to be there because godliness is one of the primary assignments of the church. All that we do must be measured by whether or not we're working on the right assignment. If we're doing great but on the wrong assignment, it's still a spiritual *F*.

Paul emphasizes this in 1 Timothy 6:3-6:

> If anyone advocates a different doctrine and does not agree with sound words, those of our Lord Jesus Christ, and with the doctrine conforming to godliness, he is conceited and understands nothing; but he has a morbid interest in controversial questions and disputes about words, out of which arise envy, strife, abusive language, evil suspicions, and constant friction between men of depraved mind and deprived of the truth, who suppose that godliness is a means of gain. But godliness actually is a means of great gain when accompanied by contentment.

GODLINESS IS A LIFESTYLE

As I've said, godliness is a lifestyle. One that reflects the character of God. But a lifestyle is not an event. Neither is it a list. A lifestyle is the way you roll. It's how you operate. It's what you think, what you choose to allow into your mind, what you say, how you view your finances, what you pursue for entertainment, and much more. You should never have to think about a lifestyle. A lifestyle is what comes natural to you. When you're living a godly life, God's character, voice, and values come through to you without your having to ask yourself *What would Jesus do?* I never understood that question when it was so popular in culture, because a spiritually mature person doesn't need to ask it. When you have an intimate relationship with Jesus, His Spirit within you guides and directs you.

Godliness assumes you agree with God internally. Now, that may sound like a simple statement, but it's much deeper and more difficult than it sounds. It can't be produced by a list or a form of religion. Agreement comes from within. When your spirit is aligned with the Holy Spirit, agreement is produced. If you're ever disagreeing with God, then you've made yourself your own idol. Once you say, *I don't think God is right on this one*, you have just judged the God who created all. You have just sought to elevate yourself above God, which puts you in the position of an idol.

A monument built to yourself, then, reflects a lifestyle of ungodliness. That's why social media can be so dangerous. It provides a platform for people to erect monuments to themselves. While it has many good uses, it often becomes nothing more than a platform for self-promotion and personal propaganda. It's one of Satan's tricks of the trade to try to elevate the human ego above God, and far too many people fall for it each and every time. Just scroll through social feeds, and you'll see it.

Another form of idolatry—or ungodliness—within the form of religion is legalism. Paul refers to this as a "doctrine of demons." We read about it in 1 Timothy 4:1-5:

> The Spirit explicitly says that in later times some will fall away from the faith, paying attention to deceitful spirits and doctrines of demons, by means of the hypocrisy of liars seared in their own conscience as with a branding iron, men who forbid marriage and advocate abstaining from foods which God has created to be gratefully shared in by those who believe and know the truth. For everything created by God is good, and nothing is to be rejected if

it is received with gratitude; for it is sanctified by means
of the word of God and prayer.

The doctrine of demons is built on the foundation of hypocrisy. So
many believers have been drawn away from a right relationship with
God because of this false doctrine. Legalism provides those in power
with a way of controlling, manipulating, and even extorting the lives
of those who fall under their care. Godliness does not mean living a
checklist-perfect life. It means living in the light of the presence of God
to such a degree that your heart beats in tune with His. Your thoughts
reflect His. Your choices honor His character. There is a consciousness
of God's presence within you when you live a godly life that affects
you. You don't need to force it or read a list of rules in order to keep it.
Your life will reflect the love of God when you make Him your priority.

LOVING GOD AND OTHERS ABOVE ALL ELSE

That's why so many people don't experience more of God's power
and victory today—they live with the rules but only visit His presence. Jesus said one rule—to love—stands paramount to all, summed
up in two expressions. He said, "'You shall love the Lord your God
with all your heart, and with all your soul, and with all your mind.'
This is the great and foremost commandment. The second is like
it; 'You shall love your neighbor as yourself'" (Matthew 22:37-39).

You are to love God and love others. Loving God means passionately pursuing His glory. When you're so closely aligned with God's
presence, love is the way you function. Love shows up in your thoughts.
Love shows up in your words. Love shows up in your choices. Love
shows up in your relationships. Love shows up in how you view and
spend time with God. Too many people spend time with God only
during the visiting hours on Sunday or for a few minutes each morning. But those who pursue godliness live in His presence.

Many people slow the speed of their driving when they see a cop car. They adjust their behavior in the light of the cop's presence. But once the cop goes a different way, they return to breaking the law by speeding. God is not interested in your obedience if it's done out of a heart that simply desires to avoid a known consequence. He desires that you obey Him because you love Him, even when no one is watching. God is always watching, and He knows what motivates us within.

GODLINESS, NOT WORLDLINESS

Holiness is a unique recognition of the light of God's presence within you. The godly person lives a life of holiness not out of obligation, but out of a desire to please God. They are aware that God is with them at all times. They are aware that God's love is their lifeforce. And because of this, they consistently view life from the lens of His kingdom perspective. They reflect Him and His influence on them like bodies of water reflect the sky. It's natural. It doesn't require effort. It flows from the stream of the Spirit's living waters within.

As I mentioned earlier, the onset of social media has opened a pandora's box of temptation toward ungodliness. One of the greatest enemies of godliness is worldliness. We read this in an exhortation Paul made to Timothy: "Avoid worldly and empty chatter, for it will lead to further ungodliness" (2 Timothy 2:16). Not only does social media offer a platform for self-promotion, but it provides Satan with a tool for worldwide *gaslighting*. Most people have heard this term, but let me define what it is for our use here:

Merriam-Webster's dictionary says gaslighting is "psychological manipulation of a person usually over an extended period of time that causes the victim to question the validity of their own thoughts, perception of reality, or memories and typically leads to confusion, loss of confidence and self-esteem, uncertainty of one's emotional or mental stability, and a dependency on the perpetrator."

Social media as well as other forms of media have for some time been used in an attempt to invalidate the concept of truth and values. The global culture at large, and Americans in particular, have been exposed to the bullying tactics of gaslighting, trying to cause us to question reality, question God's role in reality, and even question the existence of truth.

Without truth, there is no godliness. Without truth, we wind up like the individuals in the book of Judges who "did what was right in [their] own eyes" (21:25). The "worldly and empty chatter" that now goes on 24/7 ad nauseum in multiple media and digital outlets and individual people's postings has contributed to the rise of mental confusion and emotional and cultural disorders. Worldliness is any system headed by Satan that leaves God out. A person does not need to be a criminal to be worldly. Worldliness is the opposite of godliness, in that it is living a life apart from God's perspective.

Another way to grasp what worldliness is comes in understanding how we define areas of life. For example, we talk about the "world of fashion," or the "world of sports," or the "world of politics." Each of these terms define a subset in society that focuses on a certain aspect. Worldliness is the subset that focuses on perspectives other than God's. Any perspective other than God's is rooted in the "doctrines of demons" (1 Timothy 4:1). You can't merge the doctrines of demons with godliness. Just like you can't merge an AM radio signal with an FM radio signal because they operate on two very different wavelengths, worldliness and godliness cannot combine.

Those who choose to flip between the two every couple of minutes or days are known in Scripture as "double-minded." Double-mindedness leads to instability, whether it's emotional instability, relational instability, financial instability, or any other kind of instability. It also denies us of God's help in overcoming life's challenges (James 1:5-8).

We are called to avoid worldly chatter in order to live godly lives. Worldly chatter is communication void of God's perspective. To live with a consistent experience of God's work in your life, you need to align your thoughts with His. Empty and worldly chatter clutters the line. It's static that keeps you from hearing God clearly.

When a caught fish is brought up out of the water and placed on a boat or the shore, it desperately and instinctively tries to suck in oxygen through water in its mouth and then through its gills, like it does in a lake or the ocean. But it can't, because this is an environment not created for it. There is no water. Trying isn't good enough and only leads to death.

When God's people leave God out yet still try to suck in the spiritual authority or the kingdom power they need in order to overcome, they're only ushering in death cycles in their life. Whether it be the death of a dream, a relationship, a career, or of anything else, trying to survive spiritually using worldliness as your oxygen will destroy you. You were made for so much more.

You were created to live the godly, spiritual life based on your connection to and relationship with Jesus Christ. This is how you experience the abundant life Christ came to supply (John 10:10). If you're a Christian, God is your environment. He supplies your power. He supplies what you need to overcome. He supplies your everything. Trying to suck in worldly and empty chatter or a worldly perspective will only cause you and those around you pain and suffering. Godliness is a lifestyle that becomes consistent with the character of God because it is a lifestyle aware of complete dependence upon God.

YOU ALREADY HAVE WHAT YOU NEED

What's more—and what should be great news for everyone reading this book—everything you need to live a godly life in Jesus has already been given to you. We see this in 2 Peter 1:3: "His divine power has granted to us everything pertaining to life and godliness, through the true knowledge of Him who called us by His own glory and excellence." All you need to become all God wants you to be is already yours. Just like babies have within them all of the DNA they need to fully develop into adults, you and I have within us all the spiritual DNA we need to fully mature into a godly Christian.

When we accepted Jesus Christ for our salvation, the Holy Spirit fertilized our human spirit. He quickened our spirit and made us alive spiritually. The problem is that the devil seeks to abort our spiritual conception. Satan seeks to stop our spiritual maturity from progressing. And in many cases, he's been successful. But that's not because believers lack what they need to grow and develop. It's because they have been enticed, confused, deceived, distressed, or distracted away from the pursuit of godliness.

But the truth is that God has not only given you the provision for your spiritual growth, but also the power to attain it.

HOW BAD DO YOU WANT IT?

If you've ever seen someone who's been sick begin to get well, you've probably noticed their appetite return. In fact, their appetite might be increased due to the many days or weeks they didn't eat. They will be famished for nutrients and food.

One of the ways you can tell a growing believer from a stagnant, worldly Christian is their spiritual appetite. How much does this person desire to know God, learn about God, pray to God, worship God, and meditate on God? A healthy appetite should come naturally. You don't have to force an appetite on a healthy person. Neither do you have to force a spiritual appetite on a godly person.

If I were to put this in sports lingo, I'd say, "How bad do you want it?" A coach can often tell which player to put in a game or draft based on how bad that player wants to win. The more they want to win, the more willing they are to put in the work, study, exercise, and practice necessary to win.

Remember what I said in an earlier chapter? Many teams who win the Super Bowl fail to repeat a win the following year because the motivation that drives a player or a team to put in the hard work and long hours to win a championship is often rooted in the desire to get there. Once they've reached that pinnacle, the necessary work is harder to put in.

Often, then, the most challenging athletes to motivate are those who have just come off a national victory of some sort. They got what they worked for, and their desire to do it again has lessened as a result. But those who want to win will put in the work. You can tell the true athlete from the one who merely plays at being an athlete. The true athlete may very well go on to win back-to-back championships. They will put in the work even when they could rest or retire on their previous accomplishment.

God wants to know how bad you want Him. How bad you want access to His spiritual authority. How bad you want to overcome that thing, person, drama, toxicity, behavior, or whatever else is keeping you down. Your desire will show up in your willingness to deny worldly gains and focus on your spiritual walk with Jesus Christ. Are you willing to skip the parties, junk food, and other distractions— like successful athletes often do—in order to position yourself for great gain? After all, "Godliness actually is a means of great gain when accompanied by contentment" (1 Timothy 6:6).

There is a profit to godliness. There is a benefit to godliness. And as we have seen in the study of the seven churches in Revelation, there is a cause-and-effect relationship tied to your relationship with God. God desires to bless you and provide you with all you need to overcome in this life. And He's told you the pathway you need to travel to receive His power—the pursuit of godliness.

12

REJOICING IN GROWTH AND ABUNDANCE

In this chapter I share some practical applications for not only pursuing godliness but for continuing to grow in godliness. Godliness, as we've said, is the assignment for the Christian life. As we draw closer to Jesus Christ and align our lives underneath His Lordship and rule, our hearts, minds, and souls ought to be godly.

But their godliness ought to also increase over time. Godliness isn't a spiritual state we simply achieve and we're done. It's an ongoing process. It's the path to the abundant life Jesus said He came to provide (John 10:10).

If you remember—or have seen reruns of—the popular TV show *The Beverly Hillbillies*, you probably recall it with fondness. It was a funny, entertaining series about Jed Clampett, a poor mountaineer who one day noticed "black gold" come bubbling up from the ground on his property in the mountains of the Ozarks. It was oil! Jed was an instant multimillionaire, and he was persuaded to pack up all of his family's belongings and relocate to Beverly Hills, California, with his daughter, Elly May; his mother-in-law, Granny; and his nephew, Jethro. Instead of living the "get-by" life as impoverished hillbillies,

they'd be living a life of luxury. They'd have access to all of the finer-
ies this world has to offer.

What kept our attention week after week was this family's challenge
to leave their "hillbilly thinking" in the hills back home. They were now
living large, but they'd brought their small thinking with them. They
were living in a new set of hills, but they were still functioning as hillbillies. Their new home offered them so much more than the life they'd
left behind, but until they learned how to access it and use it for what
it was worth, they were stuck in a limited mindset. They seemed happy
in their own skin just the same, but shouldn't they have wanted more?

Everyone who's accepted Jesus Christ as their personal Savior
has been transferred from a place of spiritual impoverishment to a
place of spiritual riches. We've been removed from the kingdom of
Satan and are now seated at the right hand of Jesus Christ in heavenly places in the spiritual realm. But we all know it's a challenge to
leave the spiritual hillbilly life behind and partake of the new spiritual realities afforded us.

In fact, we all know what it is to bring the old life into our new
reality. The old way of thinking and the old way of living, when
brought into our new spiritual wealth and perspective, bring about
consequences. They reduce the amount of kingdom power we have
access to. They prevent us from truly living as the overcomers we are
created to be. They reduce our impact for the cause of Christ.

You and I are multimillionaires when it comes to the spiritual
realm, but far too many of us live in spiritual poverty. The time to
change that is now. The time to level up and express your full divine
destiny is now. The time to overcome all that holds you back is now.

As a reminder from the previous chapter, godliness is our ticket
to overcoming. And I define godliness as a lifestyle consistent with
the character of God. Now, godliness does not mean perfection. But
it does mean consistency carried out in such a way that it becomes
normative for us to pursue godliness as well as to quickly recognize

when we're not. God's goal for us as believers while on earth is to transform us into the image of His Son (Romans 8:29; 2 Corinthians 3:17-18). And for us to be like Jesus more and more, we need to continue to grow in godliness.

Let's look at practical applications for not just pursuing godliness but to also grow in godliness, detailed under these two general headings: doing the work and abiding with Jesus. They are both all along the path to the abundant life Jesus would have for us.

DOING THE WORK

We do not attain true godliness through human effort. It comes through supernatural enablement. God is the power Source for our godliness and spiritual growth. And we access His supernatural power through intimacy with Him and His Word.

First Timothy 4:4-10 tells it like this:

> Everything created by God is good, and nothing is to be rejected if it is received with gratitude; for it is sanctified by means of the word of God and prayer. In pointing out these things to the brethren, you will be a good servant of Christ Jesus, constantly nourished on the words of the faith and of the sound doctrine which you have been following. But have nothing to do with worldly fables fit only for old women. On the other hand, discipline yourself for the purpose of godliness; for bodily discipline is only of little profit, but godliness is profitable for all things, since it holds promise for the present life and also for the life to come. It is a trustworthy statement deserving full acceptance. For it is for this we labor and strive, because we have fixed our hope on the living God, who is the Savior of all men, especially of believers.

Paul is writing to Timothy about the need to integrate personal discipline into our lives if we want to pursue and grow in godliness. He says we are to discipline ourselves for the purpose of godliness. The Greek word for discipline is the word from which we also get our English word *gymnasium*. What do you do in a gymnasium? You work out. You get in shape. You develop your physical power.

Keep in mind, you don't go to a gym to create muscles; you go there to build the muscles you already have. The gym is designed to develop your existing physical attributes. Paul contrasts your gym experience for your physical body to your development experience for your spiritual growth. And as is true with any gym, you have to use it in order to gain benefits from it.

It's possible to have a gym membership but not get any benefit from it. The point of the gym is to offer you the opportunity to invest in your own physical development, but if you don't use it consistently, you won't gain any benefit from it. Similarly, spiritual growth will not give you the kingdom power and authority you need unless you regularly apply personal discipline to pursue and live out godliness. It doesn't come by virtue of your salvation. Spiritual growth and godliness come by virtue of your pursuit.

Did you know you already have godliness within you? When you became a Christian, you received a membership card giving you access to a spiritual gymnasium for the purpose of developing the godliness already present within you. You already possess all you need for godliness, but it does need to be developed and strengthened. God desires that you get your soul in shape. This is done through regular spiritual exercise, also referred to as spiritual disciplines.

As you know, when you use a washing machine, you still have work to do. A washing machine is a great improvement to domestic life, but it doesn't do everything. You have to cooperate with it. That is, the washing machine won't gather the dirty clothes for you. Nor will it put in its own detergent. You need to put in the detergent. You put in the bleach. You choose the water temperature and length of time it should run. The washing machine is the power that pulls off the cleanliness your clothes need, but it doesn't act alone.

As a Christian, your soul is still living in the flesh that can produce ungodly thinking, ungodly appetites, and ungodly actions. Our soul's natural tendencies and gravitational pulls require a cleansing. This cleansing occurs through the exercise and training in the spiritual gym God has provided for our move toward and ongoing pursuit of godliness. The reason so many Christians remain defeated for so long—day after day, week after week, and month after month—is that their souls are simply out of shape.

Here are four specific ways you can do the work.

1. Exercise Your Soul

Just as a body can get out of shape, which then lends itself to a lot of huffing and puffing if you need to climb sets of stairs, the soul can get out of shape too. An out-of-shape soul cannot handle what life and a sinful environment often throw at us. The way to overcome, then, is to exercise your soul. Just as you can't feed your body unhealthy food filled with toxins or preservatives and expect it to be at its optimum performance level, you can't feed your soul the toxins of this world and expect to live as a kingdom overcomer.

We all know that with regard to our physical bodies, eating healthy or starting an exercise regimen always begins with a decision. You have to decide to do it. The reality is that a lot of times a person who works out—even if it's just a walking regimen—or eats healthy doesn't want to do it. They don't always feel like it. But they continue to do it because their optimal health is more important than their emotions. Or even fatigue. When they prioritize doing something about their fatigue through strengthening their bodies, despite how they feel at the start, they're making what we call a "priority decision." A priority decision means something you determine to do whether or not you feel like doing it. It is your priority.

If your soul is out of shape because ungodliness rules your thoughts, words, and actions, you need more than an intention to overcome. You need more than a resolution to live as an overcomer. You need more than a desire to grow spiritually. If spiritual laziness overrules decisions and discipline that develop your spiritual muscles, then you will not be positioned to overcome difficulties as a way of life. You need more than a good intention to overcome. You need to put in the work.

2. Deny Worldliness

As we've already seen, the enemy of godliness is worldliness. Paul reemphasizes this in the 1 Timothy passage we just read. He said we are to relinquish "worldly fables fit for old women." That phrase from the culture of the time means we are to reject what has no biblical or spiritual foundation tied to it. Paul even talks about some of those things in the first three verses of 1 Timothy chapter 4:

> The Spirit explicitly says that in later times some will fall away from the faith, paying attention to deceitful spirits and doctrines of demons, by means of the hypocrisy of liars seared in their own conscience as with a branding iron, men who forbid marriage and advocate abstaining from foods which God has created to be gratefully shared in by those who believe and know the truth (1 Timothy 4:1-3).

Worldly fables refers to false teachings aimed at keeping you from being godly (or even continuing to grow in godliness). They are sayings and discussions with no biblical foundation or truth. Paul gives us two examples in the passage: forbidding marriage and forbidding foods. He refers to both as doctrines of demons. They are a lot of chatter with no divine authority.

Essentially, Paul lets us know that anyone who chooses to live their life on fables with no biblical foundation cannot expect life transformation to occur. Life transformation takes place when you practice the spiritual disciplines. You develop your ability to overcome when you base your perspective on God's kingdom worldview. You already possess all you need to live in and grow in godliness, but you need to refrain from mixing it with worldly ways of thought.

3. Live in Community

One of the best ways to keep up a workout program is to have a workout partner. Then you have someone to help you stay motivated when you don't feel like working out, and you'll do the same for them. A workout partner creates accountability. Also, workout partners spot you to help you overcome the heaviness of the weights you're seeking to lift.

It's so important to invest in the spiritual growth of others if you want to grow spiritually yourself. We grow better together. That's why church membership is so important. If you aren't regularly attending church somewhere, I encourage you to find a church home where you can grow under the teaching of the pastor and alongside the other members. The Christian life is not the solitary life. We were built for community.

4. Develop Gratitude

You need to visit the godliness gym on a regular basis, because godliness is profitable and beneficial for every aspect of your life right now. Godliness benefits your finances, relationships, marriage, parenting, career, and even your physical health. If and when you get the godliness workout going strong, you'll experience the benefits everywhere. God longs for you to live a whole life complete with all you need to overcome—the abundant life. He wants to see you successful in all you do.

In fact, as we read earlier, God has equipped you for success: "Everything created by God is good, and nothing is to be rejected if it is received with gratitude; for it is sanctified by means of the word of God and prayer" (1 Timothy 4:5). Keep in mind, "everything" means nothing is excluded.

Everything good that comes into your life comes from God. There are no exceptions. If it is beneficial to you, then it is derived from God as the Source. It is to be received with gratitude while simultaneously being sanctified. You sanctify what God has given you through gratitude. That's a foundational part of your spiritual workout routine: thankfulness.

Thankfulness isn't something we do once a year when eating a turkey. Thankfulness is to be part of our daily way of life. When we are grateful to God, we are inviting in God's presence at a greater level. It is bringing God to bear on all you do. To sanctify something means to set it apart through the Word of God in prayer. You are to make it special through a prayerful heart based on God's Word and filled with gratitude.

Let's take the act of "saying grace" as an example. Often when people eat, they bless their meals. It may be the same prayer said the same way, but the point of it is a "blessing." What they're seeking to do is sanctify the food and bring it underneath God's creative power.

The problem is that we say grace so easily for our food, but we forget to bless everything else. We forget to show gratitude. We forget to recognize that it is God who sits above it all and is responsible for all the good things we have. What Paul is reminding us in 1 Timothy 4:5 is that we are to practice the spiritual discipline of gratitude in all we do. We are to invite God's presence into all we do. That's what it means to "abide."

ABIDING WITH JESUS

Jesus said to His disciples and to us, "If you abide in Me, and My words abide in you, ask whatever you wish, and it will be done for you. My Father is glorified by this, that you bear much fruit, and so prove to be My disciples. Just as the Father has loved Me, I have also loved you; abide in My love" (John 15:7-9).

Jesus is the dispenser of godliness. Your level of godliness comes from your level of abiding in Christ. Jesus is the One who produces the spiritual fruit in you. You tap into His power to produce godliness in you by practicing His presence in your life.

Practicing the presence of Jesus means bringing Him in on everything you do, whether in your thoughts, words, or actions. It also includes showing a heart of gratitude throughout your day as you witness and identify the many provisions Jesus has given you. Whether it's a provision of wisdom to know what to say or do at the right time, or the provision of safety, or even a material provision, Jesus is the Source of all good things in your life. You sanctify these things through the Word of God and prayer.

What would happen to a weight lifter who only lifted a few times a month for an hour? Inevitably his muscles would deteriorate over time. Abiding with Jesus on a Sunday here or there is not the equivalent of a spiritual workout regimen. Abiding means you are continually and purposefully placing yourself in Christ's presence throughout your life.

Far too often, I see people come to church only in search of a blessing or a bailout—more money, a better marriage, or something else to improve their lives. But there's a problem with that mentality. When you come to church just for a blessing or a bailout, but you don't authentically care about pursuing godliness as a lifestyle, you'll likely not experience your blessing or bailout. God's provision is often tied to spiritual power, and spiritual power is gained through a pursuit of godliness. Godliness comes through a close abiding with Jesus Christ coupled with a consistent practice of the spiritual disciplines of applying God's Word, praying, and offering thanks.

Godliness involves more than daily devotions or attending a Bible study. That has its place. But again, godliness is a way of life, a lifestyle. When you abide with Jesus as a way of life, based on His Word and in regular communication with Him, you no longer allow the doctrines of demons to dominate you. You no longer allow worldly fables or empty chatter to siphon off your energy and your time. In fact, you begin to feel uncomfortable with these things when exposed to them, because your spirit recognizes the demonic influence behind them all.

You can tell you're growing in godliness when ungodliness, whether your own or someone else's, becomes increasingly uncomfortable. You can't watch some of the same shows as easily as before. You can't listen to some of the same music you used to, as the lyrics start to stand out to you for what they are. You can't even hang with some of the same friends you used to, as your eyes become open to their worldly patterns and lack of spiritual focus in what they say and do. Your life is truly transformed from the inside out when you pursue godliness in the gym of spiritual growth.

We all have what we need to live as overcomers. We have our spiritual workout plan, and it boils down to bringing Jesus to bear on all we think, say, and do. You are to practice His presence all day, every day. Sometimes it will be one minute during something you're focused on. Other times it will be five minutes when you really seek to tap into His spirit in the midst of your day. Other times you may find yourself speaking audibly to Jesus as you're working through a decision.

However it looks for you, and it will look different for each of us, you will know you're growing as you see yourself overcoming what used to hold you back or defeat you. You grow as you develop a deeper, more intimate relationship with Jesus Christ and no longer rely on the rules and rituals of religion.

God's got a gym membership for you. And, by the way, it's open enrollment. Anyone who wants to get in can do so by virtue of your relationship with Jesus Christ. He has already paid the price. With this membership and use of it comes the power of God's Word to operate in your life through prayer and gratitude as you practice the presence of Christ. While godliness grows within you, godlessness will have to shrink and fall away. You can't have both. The overcomer's life is a life of spiritual discipline revealed by godliness in all you think, say, and do. But the good part is that it's not entirely up to you. You have help.

When I was growing up in Baltimore, I loved to eat ice cream. But I'm a soft ice cream kind of guy, so I didn't enjoy hard ice cream. And I didn't have a microwave around. So I learned to mash my ice cream with a spoon until it softened. But as an adult, I have a microwave, and now instead of doing all of the hard work of mashing my ice cream to soften it, I just lift the ice cream container's lid, then place the container in the microwave for a few seconds. The microwave does all of the work I used to have to do. By putting my ice cream in an environment that does the work for me, I get to rest and enjoy what I love without the pain of the effort.

I don't know how long you've been mashing this life with a spoon, trying to soften the hard edges it brings. I don't know how stuck you've become along the way. But I do know that there is a microwave named Jesus, and if you'll allow your spirit to hang out in Him, He will soften things for you. He will smooth things for you. He will sweeten things for you. He will satisfy you with good things as you tap into His spiritual power for you to live as an overcomer in Christ, striving for godliness and the abundant life along the way, and be rewarded for it in eternity.

FROM VICTIM TO VICTOR

One of the popular entertainment sports today is professional wrestling. The audience is enthralled as combatants hurl, pound, tackle, and pin each other in the ring. But many people don't know these matches are scripted. That is, the winner is determined prior to the conflict. When the two are in the ring battling, then, the predetermined winner is not actually fighting *for* victory but fighting *from* victory. Yes, the victors still have to go through the process of battle that can leave them bruised, battered, and bloody, but they know they'll emerge victorious when all is said and done.

I have good news for you. If you know Jesus Christ as your Savior, your victory as an overcomer has already been predetermined. In whatever conflict you're facing, you're not fighting *for* victory; you're fighting *from* victory. Yes, you'll have to go through the battles of life since the world, the flesh, and Satan still war against you. But be of good cheer. As you follow Jesus as Lord, He will give you the strength and power to recover and go on.

So if the problems in your life seem to be winning, just remember you're already a victor. Sometimes wrestlers appear to be headed toward defeat, but then the battle takes a turn and they emerge a victor. Even if your troubles are victimizing you, you are not a victim.

You are actually a victor in waiting. So hold up your head, leave the corner of defeat, and claim your predetermined victory in Christ.

Most of all, remember that "greater is He who is in you than he who is in the world" (1 John 4:4). That's the mindset of an overcomer.

APPENDIXES

SCRIPTURES FOR ENCOURAGEMENT TO OVERCOME

These things I have spoken to you, so that in Me you may have peace. In the world you have tribulation, but take courage; I have overcome the world.

JOHN 16:33

Whatever is born of God overcomes the world; and this is the victory that has overcome the world—our faith.

1 JOHN 5:4

You are from God, little children, and have overcome them; because greater is He who is in you than he who is in the world.

1 JOHN 4:4

Who is the one who overcomes the world, but he who believes that Jesus is the Son of God?

1 JOHN 5:5

*He who overcomes, I will grant to him to sit down
with Me on My throne, as I also overcame and
sat down with My Father on His throne.*

REVELATION 3:21

*Trust in the LORD with all your heart and do not lean on
your own understanding. In all your ways acknowledge
Him, and He will make your paths straight.*

PROVERBS 3:5-6

*They overcame him because of the blood of the Lamb
and because of the word of their testimony, and they
did not love their life even when faced with death.*

REVELATION 12:11

Submit therefore to God. Resist the devil and he will flee from you.

JAMES 4:7

*No temptation has overtaken you but such as is common to
man; and God is faithful, who will not allow you to be tempted
beyond what you are able, but with the temptation will provide
the way of escape also, so that you will be able to endure it.*

1 CORINTHIANS 10:13

*In all these things we overwhelmingly
conquer through Him who loved us.*

ROMANS 8:37

*No one who is born of God practices sin, because His seed
abides in him; and he cannot sin, because he is born of God.*

1 JOHN 3:9

*I have been crucified with Christ; and it is no longer
I who live, but Christ lives in me; and the life which
I now live in the flesh I live by faith in the Son of
God, who loved me and gave Himself up for me.*

GALATIANS 2:20

*Thanks be to God, who gives us the victory
through our Lord Jesus Christ.*

1 CORINTHIANS 15:57

Do not be overcome by evil, but overcome evil with good.

ROMANS 12:21

*He has said to me, "My grace is sufficient for you, for power is
perfected in weakness." Most gladly, therefore, I will rather boast
about my weaknesses, so that the power of Christ may dwell in me.*

2 CORINTHIANS 12:9

*The LORD is my light and my salvation; whom shall I fear?
The LORD is the defense of my life; whom shall I dread?*

PSALM 27:1

*He who overcomes, and he who keeps My deeds until the
end, to him I will give authority over the nations.*

REVELATION 2:26

*Peace I leave with you; My peace I give to you; not
as the world gives do I give to you. Do not let your
heart be troubled, nor let it be fearful.*

JOHN 14:27

He who overcomes will thus be clothed in white garments;
and I will not erase his name from the book of life, and I will
confess his name before My Father and before His angels.

REVELATION 3:5

I am writing to you, fathers, because you know Him who
has been from the beginning. I am writing to you, young
men, because you have overcome the evil one. I have
written to you, children, because you know the Father.

1 JOHN 2:13

It is better to be humble in spirit with the lowly
than to divide the spoil with the proud.

PROVERBS 16:19

Do not be conformed to this world, but be transformed by the
renewing of your mind, so that you may prove what the will
of God is, that which is good and acceptable and perfect.

ROMANS 12:2

The Light shines in the darkness, and the
darkness did not comprehend it.

JOHN 1:5

Fight the good fight of faith; take hold of the eternal
life to which you were called, and you made the good
confession in the presence of many witnesses.

1 TIMOTHY 6:12

Whoever believes that Jesus is the Christ is born of God, and
whoever loves the Father loves the child born of Him.

1 JOHN 5:1

I am the LORD your God, who upholds your right hand,
who says to you, "Do not fear, I will help you."

ISAIAH 41:13

Since we have so great a cloud of witnesses surrounding
us, let us also lay aside every encumbrance and
the sin which so easily entangles us, and let us run
with endurance the race that is set before us.

HEBREWS 12:1

Nothing will be impossible with God.

LUKE 1:37

Be of sober spirit, be on the alert. Your adversary, the devil,
prowls around like a roaring lion, seeking someone to devour.

1 PETER 5:8

We know that no one who is born of God sins; but He who was
born of God keeps him, and the evil one does not touch him.

1 JOHN 5:18

Behold, an hour is coming, and has already come, for you to
be scattered, each to his own home, and to leave Me alone;
and yet I am not alone, because the Father is with Me.

JOHN 16:32

*He who overcomes will inherit these things, and
I will be his God and he will be My son.*

REVELATION 21:7

*Be anxious for nothing, but in everything by prayer and
supplication with thanksgiving let your requests be made known
to God. And the peace of God, which surpasses all comprehension,
will guard your hearts and your minds in Christ Jesus.*

PHILIPPIANS 4:6-7

I can do all things through Him who strengthens me.

PHILIPPIANS 4:13

*You, O LORD, are a shield about me, My
glory, and the One who lifts my head.*

PSALM 3:3

*If anyone is in Christ, he is a new creature; the old
things passed away; behold, new things have come.*

2 CORINTHIANS 5:17

*We know that God causes all things to work
together for good to those who love God, to those
who are called according to His purpose.*

ROMANS 8:28

*Consider it all joy, my brethren, when you encounter various
trials, knowing that the testing of your faith produces
endurance. And let endurance have its perfect result, so that
you may be perfect and complete, lacking in nothing.*

JAMES 1:2-4

Casting all your anxiety on Him, because He cares for you.

1 PETER 5:7

This you know, my beloved brethren. But everyone must be quick to hear, slow to speak and slow to anger; for the anger of man does not achieve the righteousness of God. Therefore, putting aside all filthiness and all that remains of wickedness, in humility receive the word implanted, which is able to save your souls.

JAMES 1:19-21

This is the love of God, that we keep His commandments; and His commandments are not burdensome.

1 JOHN 5:3

If we confess our sins, He is faithful and righteous to forgive us our sins and to cleanse us from all unrighteousness.

1 JOHN 1:9

Do not be eager in your heart to be angry, for anger resides in the bosom of fools.

ECCLESIASTES 7:9

He who restrains his words has knowledge, and he who has a cool spirit is a man of understanding.

PROVERBS 17:27

Judgment is upon this world; now the ruler of this world will be cast out.

JOHN 12:31

Our struggle is not against flesh and blood, but against the rulers, against the powers, against the world forces of this darkness, against the spiritual forces of wickedness in the heavenly places.

EPHESIANS 6:12

God so loved the world, that He gave His only begotten Son, that whoever believes in Him shall not perish, but have eternal life. For God did not send the Son into the world to judge the world, but that the world might be saved through Him.

JOHN 3:16-17

Trust in the LORD with all your heart and do not lean on your own understanding.

PROVERBS 3:5

The one who does not love does not know God, for God is love.

1 JOHN 4:8

There is no fear in love; but perfect love casts out fear, because fear involves punishment, and the one who fears is not perfected in love.

1 JOHN 4:18

God has not given us a spirit of timidity, but of power and love and discipline.

2 TIMOTHY 1:7

Let us draw near with confidence to the throne of grace, so that we may receive mercy and find grace to help in time of need.

HEBREWS 4:16

Seek the LORD and His strength; seek His face continually.

1 CHRONICLES 16:11

Having been justified by faith, we have peace with God through our Lord Jesus Christ, through whom also we have obtained our introduction by faith into this grace in which we stand; and we exult in hope of the glory of God.

ROMANS 5:1-2

This is the confidence which we have before Him, that, if we ask anything according to His will, He hears us.

1 JOHN 5:14

He who believes in the Son has eternal life; but he who does not obey the Son will not see life, but the wrath of God abides on him.

JOHN 3:36

He was telling them a parable to show that at all times they ought to pray and not to lose heart.

LUKE 18:1

I consider that the sufferings of this present time are not worthy to be compared with the glory that is to be revealed to us.

ROMANS 8:18

Beloved, let us love one another, for love is from God; and everyone who loves is born of God and knows God.

1 JOHN 4:7

*Have I not commanded you? Be strong and
courageous! Do not tremble or be dismayed, for the
L*ORD *your God is with you wherever you go.*

JOSHUA 1:9

*In all these things we overwhelmingly
conquer through Him who loved us.*

ROMANS 8:37

*Do not fear, for I am with you;
do not anxiously look about you, for I am your God.
I will strengthen you, surely I will help you, surely I
will uphold you with My righteous right hand.*

ISAIAH 41:10

*Be strong and courageous, do not be afraid or tremble
at them, for the L*ORD *your God is the one who goes
with you. He will not fail you or forsake you.*

DEUTERONOMY 31:6

*All Scripture is inspired by God and profitable for teaching,
for reproof, for correction, for training in righteousness.*

2 TIMOTHY 3:16

THE URBAN ALTERNATIVE

The Urban Alternative (TUA) equips, empowers, and unites Christians to impact individuals, families, churches, and communities through a thoroughly kingdom-agenda worldview. In teaching truth, we seek to transform lives.

The core cause of the problems we face in our personal lives, homes, churches, and societies is a spiritual one. Therefore, the only way to address that core cause is spiritually. We've tried a political, social, economic, and even a religious agenda, and now it's time for a kingdom agenda.

The kingdom agenda can be defined as the visible manifestation of the comprehensive rule of God over every area of life.

The unifying central theme throughout the Bible is the glory of God and the advancement of His kingdom. The conjoining thread from Genesis to Revelation—from beginning to end—is focused on one thing: God's glory through advancing God's kingdom.

When we do not recognize that theme, the Bible becomes for us a series of disconnected stories that are great for inspiration but seem to be unrelated in purpose and direction. Understanding the role of the kingdom in Scripture increases our understanding of the relevancy of this several-thousand-year-old text to our day-to-day living. That's because God's kingdom was not only then; it is now.

The absence of the kingdom's influence in our personal lives, family lives, churches, and communities has led to a deterioration in our world of immense proportions:

- People live segmented, compartmentalized lives because they lack God's kingdom worldview.

- Families disintegrate because they exist for their own satisfaction rather than for the kingdom.

- Churches are limited in the scope of their impact because they fail to comprehend that the goal of the church is not the church itself but the kingdom.

- Communities have nowhere to turn to find real solutions for real people who have real problems because the church has become divided, in-grown, and unable to transform the cultural and political landscape in any relevant way.

By optimizing the solutions of heaven, the kingdom agenda offers us a way to see and live life with a solid hope. When God is no longer the final and authoritative standard under which all else falls, order and hope have left with Him. But the reverse of that is true as well: as long as we have God, we have hope. If God is still in the picture, and as long as His agenda is still on the table, it's not over.

Even if relationships collapse, God will sustain us. Even if finances dwindle, God will keep us. Even if dreams die, God will revive us. As long as God and His rule are still the overarching standard in our lives, families, churches, and communities, there is always hope.

Our world needs the King's agenda. Our churches need the King's agenda. Our families need the King's agenda.

We've put together a three-part plan to direct us to heal the divisions and strive for unity as we move toward the goal of truly being one nation under God. This three-part plan calls us to assemble with others in unity, to address the issues that divide us, and to act together for social impact. Following this plan, we will see individuals, families, churches, and communities transformed as we follow God's kingdom agenda in every area of our lives. You can request this plan by texting the keyword "strategy" to 55659 or visiting TonyEvans.org/strategy.

In many major cities, drivers can take a loop to the other side of the city when they don't want to head straight through downtown. This loop takes them close enough to the city center so they can see its towering buildings and skyline but not close enough to actually experience it.

This is precisely what we, as a culture, have done with God. We have put Him on the "loop" of our personal, family, church, and community lives. He's close enough to be at hand should we need Him in an emergency but far enough away that He can't be the center of who we are. We want God on the "loop," not the King of the Bible who comes downtown into the very heart of our ways. And as we have seen in our own lives and in the lives of others, leaving God on the "loop" brings about dire consequences.

But when we make God, and His rule, the centerpiece of all we think, do, or say, we experience Him in the way He longs for us to experience Him. He wants us to be kingdom people with kingdom minds set on fulfilling His kingdom's purposes. He wants us to pray, as Jesus did, "Not My will, but Thy will be done" because His is the kingdom, the power, and the glory.

There is only one God, and we are not Him. As King and Creator, God calls the shots. Only when we align ourselves under His comprehensive hand will we access His full power and authority in all spheres of life: personal, familial, ecclesiastical, and governmental.

As we learn how to govern ourselves under God, we then transform the institutions of family, church, and society using a biblically based kingdom worldview.

Under Him, we touch heaven and change earth.

To achieve our goal, we use a variety of strategies, approaches, and resources for reaching and equipping as many people as possible.

BROADCAST MEDIA

Millions of individuals experience *The Alternative with Dr. Tony Evans*, a daily broadcast on nearly 2,000 radio outlets and in more than 130 countries. The broadcast can also be seen on several television networks including TBN and Fox Business and is available online at TonyEvans.org. You can also listen to or view the daily broadcast by downloading the Tony Evans app for free in the App Store. More than 60,000,000 message downloads/streams occur each year.

LEADERSHIP TRAINING

The *Tony Evans Training Center* (TETC) facilitates a comprehensive discipleship platform, which provides an educational program that embodies the ministry philosophy of Dr. Tony Evans as expressed through the kingdom agenda. The training courses focus on leadership development and discipleship in the following five tracks:

1. Bible & Theology

2. Personal Growth

3. Family and Relationships

4. Church Health and Leadership Development

5. Society and Community Impact Strategies

The TETC program includes courses for both local and online students. Furthermore, TETC programming includes course work for nonstudent attendees. Pastors, Christian leaders, and Christian laity—both local and at a distance—can seek out the Kingdom Agenda Certificate for personal, spiritual, and professional development. For more information, visit TonyEvansTraining.org.

Kingdom Agenda Pastors (KAP) provides a viable network for like-minded pastors who embrace the kingdom agenda philosophy. Pastors have the opportunity to go deeper with Dr. Tony Evans as they are given greater biblical knowledge, practical applications, and resources to impact individuals, families, churches, and communities. KAP welcomes senior and associate pastors of all churches. KAP also offers an annual Summit held each year in Dallas with intensive seminars, workshops, and resources. For more information, visit KAFellowship.org.

Pastors' Wives Ministry, founded by the late Dr. Lois Evans, provides counsel, encouragement, and spiritual resources for pastors' wives as they serve with their husbands in the ministry. A primary focus of the ministry is the KAP Summit, where senior pastors' wives have a safe place to reflect, renew, and relax along with receiving training in personal development, spiritual growth, and care for their emotional and physical well-being. For more information, visit LoisEvans.org.

KINGDOM COMMUNITY IMPACT

The outreach programs of The Urban Alternative seek to provide positive impact on individuals, churches, families, and communities through a variety of ministries. We see these efforts as necessary to our calling as a ministry and essential to the communities we serve. With training on how to initiate and maintain programs to adopt schools, provide homeless services, and partner toward unity and justice with the local police precincts, which creates a connection between the police and our community, we, as a ministry, live out God's kingdom agenda according to our *Kingdom Strategy for Community Transformation.*

The *Kingdom Strategy for Community Transformation* is a three-part plan that equips churches to have a positive impact on their communities for the kingdom of God. It also provides numerous practical suggestions for how this three-part plan can be implemented in your community, and it serves as a blueprint for unifying churches around the common goal of creating a better world for all of us. For more information, visit TonyEvans.org, then click on the link to access the 3-Point Plan. A course for this strategy is also offered online through the Tony Evans Training Center.

Tony Evans Films ushers in positive life change through compelling video-shorts, animation, and feature-length films. We seek to build kingdom disciples through the power of story. We use a variety of platforms for viewer consumption and have 220,000,000+ digital views. We also merge video-shorts and film with relevant Bible study materials to bring people to the saving knowledge of Jesus Christ and to strengthen the body of Christ worldwide. Tony Evans Films released its first feature-length film, *Kingdom Men Rising,* in April 2019 in more than 800 theaters nationwide in partnership with Lifeway Films. The second release, *Journey with Jesus,* is in partnership with Right-Now Media and was released for three nights of nearly 1,000 sold-out theaters in November 2021. The third release is *Unbound: The Bible's Journey Through History,* a documentary focusing on the transmission of the Bible from the third through the sixteenth centuries.

RESOURCE DEVELOPMENT

By providing a variety of published materials, we are fostering lifelong learning partnerships with the people we serve. Dr. Evans has published more than 125 unique titles based on more than 50 years of preaching—in booklet, book, or Bible study format. He also holds the honor of writing and publishing the first full-Bible commentary and study Bible by an African American, released in 2019. This Bible sits in permanent display as a historic release in the Museum of the Bible in Washington, DC.

For more information, and to opt-in to Dr. Evans' devotional email, text the word "DEVO" to 55659, call (800) 800-3222, or visit us online at:

www.TonyEvans.org/devo

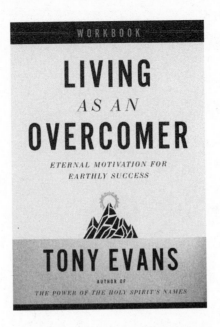

SAY GOODBYE TO LUKEWARM FAITH

This workbook companion to Dr. Tony Evans' *Living as an Overcomer DVD* helps you dive deeper into Christ's message to the seven churches in the book of Revelation. In the face of growing cultural hostility and the church's own spiritual decay, you will examine the practical ways this powerful section of Scripture leads you to

- reassess your life's priorities and recommit to your first love in Jesus

- cultivate genuine faith, even when life comes at you hard

- turn away from lukewarm faith, and authentically submit to Christ's standard

Experience victory over sin and lay claim to all God has in store for you. As this study guides you to listen to God's Word and put it into practice, you will discover that there is no obstacle, habit, or situation you face that Jesus hasn't already given you the power to overcome.

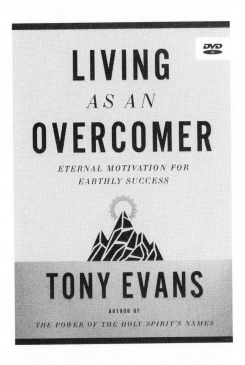

BE CHALLENGED TO LIVE TRIUMPHANTLY

God has already revealed everything we need to know to experience victory over sin. In the sessions from the *Living as an Overcomer DVD*, Dr. Evans helps you triumph over life's difficulties by taking heed of Christ's message to the seven churches in Revelation.

Throughout these lessons, Dr. Evans helps you rekindle your deepest convictions and strengthen your spiritual commitment as Christ calls you to return to His love. Get ready to vanquish obstacles and prevail in your present circumstances by laying claim to all that God has in store for you.

While the unique hardships of our modern lives can often feel insurmountable, you will discover how Jesus' message to some of the earliest churches brims with power and relevance, even in our contemporary context.

 **EVANS**
THE URBAN ALTERNATIVE

Building kingdom disciples.

At **The Urban Alternative,** our heart is to build kingdom disciples—a vision that starts with the individual and expands to the family, the church and the nation. The nearly 50-year teaching ministry of Tony Evans has allowed us to reach a world in need with:

The Alternative – Our flagship radio program brings hope and comfort to an audience of millions on over 1,400 radio outlets across the country.

tonyevans.org – Our library of teaching resources provides solid Bible teaching through the inspirational books and sermons of Tony Evans.

Tony Evans Training Center –
Experience the adventure of God's Word with our online classroom, providing at-your-own-pace courses for your PC or mobile device. Visit tonyevanstraining.org.

Tony Evans app – This popular resource for finding inspiration on-the-go has had over 20,000,000 launches. It's packed with audio and video clips, devotionals, Scripture readings and dozens of other tools.

tonyevans.org

Life is busy,
but Bible study is still possible.

To learn more about Harvest House books and
to read sample chapters, visit our website:

www.HarvestHousePublishers.com

HARVEST HOUSE PUBLISHERS
EUGENE, OREGON